Dogs and Cats
Have Souls Too

ALSO BY JENNY SMEDLEY:

Past Life Angels

Past Life (meditation CD)

Souls Don't Lie

The Tree That Talked

How to Be Happy

Forever Faithful

Supernaturally True

Pets Have Souls Too

Angel Whispers

Soul Angels

Everyday Angels

Pets Are Forever

Angels Please Hear Me

A Year with the Angels

My Angel Diary 2012

An Angel by Your Side

Soul Mates

My Angel Diary 2013

My Angel Diary 2014

ry 2015

aling

ry 2017

Angel Stories

Dogs and Cats Have Souls Too

Incredible True Stories of Pets Who Heal, Protect and Communicate

JENNY SMEDLEY

HAY HOUSE

Carlsbad, California • New York City
London • Sydney • New Delhi

Published in the United Kingdom by:
Hay House UK Ltd, Astley House, 33 Notting Hill Gate, London W11 3JQ
Tel: +44 (0)20 3675 2450; Fax: +44 (0)20 3675 2451
www.hayhouse.co.uk

Published in the United States of America by:
Hay House Inc., PO Box 5100, Carlsbad, CA 92018-5100
Tel: (1) 760 431 7695 or (800) 654 5126
Fax: (1) 760 431 6948 or (800) 650 5115
www.hayhouse.com

Published in Australia by:
Hay House Australia Ltd, 18/36 Ralph St, Alexandria NSW 2015
Tel: (61) 2 9669 4299; Fax: (61) 2 9669 4144
www.hayhouse.com.au

Published and distributed in India by:
Hay House Publishers India, Muskaan Complex, Plot No.3, B-2,
Vasant Kunj, New Delhi 110 070
Tel: (91) 11 4176 1620; Fax: (91) 11 4176 1630
www.hayhouse.co.in

A catalogue record for this book is available from the British Library.

ISBN: 978-1-78817-065-9

Interior images: 1 Shutterstock/cynoclub/Eric Isselee/photomaster; 33, 175 Shutterstock/Africa Studio; 45 Shutterstock/Oleksandr Lytvynenko; 59 123 RF; 95, 231 Shutterstock/Grigorita Ko; 109 Shutterstock/Olena Brodetska; 125 123RF/Susan Richey-Schmitz; 151 Shutterstock/TheRocky41; 201 Shutterstock/CebotariN; 217 Shutterstock/Vasek Rak; 243 Shutterstock/vvvita

Printed and bound in Great Britain by TJ International, Padstow, Cornwall.

MIX
Paper from
responsible sources
FSC
www.fsc.org   FSC® C013056

Contents

Foreword

Jenny Smedley is already a name known to animal lovers worldwide, but for those to whom her name is new, let me explain a little. Her thesis – that animals have souls as well as humans – can easily be mistaken for a piece of pure 'sentimentality'. But the lightness and humour of many of the anecdotes in this book belie a subtext which is the power behind a very important and growing revolution in our attitude to the other species on Planet Earth. In my work for Animal Welfare in recent months, I have been struck by a very clear insight. We all grow up, and leave home, and are sure that our system of beliefs is entirely our own, supported by verifiable evidence and logical argument. But for the vast majority of us, nothing could be further from the truth. We don't have to look very far into our everyday behaviour to see that it is dominated by habit – a whole system of behaviour patterns learned from our parents or guardians in our early childhood, only marginally modified by ourselves, often in response to pressure from our peers in later life.

These behaviours are based on mainly unquestioned beliefs, and many of them relate to the way we treat animals. Many of us eat the flesh of animals daily, reassured by the echoes of our parents' voices in our heads: 'You need your protein' … 'It's good for you' … etc. In spite of mountains of clear evidence that a vegetarian diet is much healthier for our bodies, much more beneficial to the health of our planet and, if adopted by all, would vastly decrease the suffering of animals, these old beliefs, and these behaviours, persist. Ah – the *suffering* of animals? Here is where we are liable to be accused of sentimentality, of anthropomorphism. Many of us in our youth were given open or implied messages such as, 'Animals don't suffer in the same way we do,' or 'Animals are there for us to use any way we want,' or 'Animals are dirty,' or 'Some animals are vicious, some are pests, vermin – must be *controlled*' or 'It's brave to kill animals.' So daily, millions upon millions of farm animals are cruelly abused, millions of animals are used in horrific experiments in the name of making humans live longer, or look prettier, and what is left of our wild animals have no rights – can be stalked, trapped, snared, shot or torn apart by men with packs of dogs. Even a quick look at all this by a visiting alien would lead him to the conclusion that the human race, while rather laughably considering itself to be more or less the only important species on the planet, comes out as the most badly behaved. The alien would conclude that our behaviours are mainly governed by instinct, and that, while we are anatomically almost indistinguishable from the other mammals on Earth, we refuse to admit their similarity to us, and refuse to recognize their right to live and breathe in peace. Jonathan Safran Foer, in his book *Eating Animals*, alerted me to a word I had not encountered before: Anthropodenial – the illogical denial of the fact that the animals around us see, hear, feel almost exactly as we do; they also feel pleasure, pain and fear, and it is the denial of these truths which licenses those lacking in empathy to try to justify the cruelty they inflict, or assent to.

All this might seem a long way away from a book which is full of lightness and joy, and insights into animal thinking, emotion and abstract thought. But as you dip into these stories, you will find constant triggers … reminders that we need to constantly question the edicts of old ways of thinking. At my Sunday School, at the age of about ten, we were taught 'only humans have souls – only humans can go to Heaven.' It bothered me for years – it seemed grossly unfair, and I fiercely resisted the notion that my cat might be turned away from the Gates of Heaven. The thought often returns to me even now. Of course, there is no evidence for that teaching at all, and it must have justified countless unnecessary acts of cruelty and neglect of animals through the ages. On every page of this book, I am reassured that it's just another old belief which needs to be thrown out of the window, for lack of evidence. No! More than that – thrown out because of clear evidence to the contrary, recounted with great skill and dedication in this book.

You can be sure of it. As Ms Smedley says… *animals have souls, too!*

Brian May

Introduction

My Journey with Animals

All through my life I've had experiences with animals, which has brought me to right where I am today. Animals have taught me such a lot: about tolerance, about unconditional love and about how in many ways they are teachers for all of us, so you can see I am very strongly connected to the animal kingdom. I have learned from these experiences that all animals have souls, so of course cats and dogs do, too.

Some sceptics will probably label me a 'bunny hugger' – all emotion and no realism. This isn't true. While I love all animals, I also respect them and their place in the scheme of things.

My belief is that animals are just as important as we are in the wide-angle view of things, and when we eradicate a species, through design or accident, we have no way of knowing what long-term effect this might have on us. Our planet, our ecosystem and our way of life are very fragile. We upset the balance at our peril. We rely heavily on some of the smallest of God's creatures for our very survival. Take pollinators, such as bees, for instance. Without their skills the keystone would soon fall out of humanity's wall, and yet their decline is being treated like something fairly trivial.

I'm also extremely saddened and upset by the growing number of young people who commit violent crimes against others, because this could so easily be stopped – I truly feel that if all children were brought up to respect and care for animals, they would grow into decent adults who cared for other people, too. I think all children should have pets but, vitally, they must be taught to look after them properly and unselfishly, and to understand that all living things feel pain and sorrow, just as they do. Yes, indeed, animals can teach humans a lot about spirituality: *Ask the animals, and they will teach you – Job 12:7-10.*

Animals were always my first love. I had a strong empathy with them right from the time I could first walk and speak. Their purity of spirit and their constant ability to love unconditionally often made me wish for a world totally populated with just animals when I was young. They didn't judge me and they responded to me with openness and honesty. It didn't matter to me whether an animal was cute and furry like a dog or a cat, spiky and prickly like a hedgehog, or derided, even hated, like a mouse or a rat. I loved them all the same. An animal doesn't care what race or colour or gender you are. Whether you are fat or thin, beautiful or ugly, poor or rich, they treat everyone the same.

My current dog, KC, told me recently, 'We're the same as you. We're just like people,' and this is the message of my book. Animals are just like us in the way they feel things, the way they share emotions and energy, and in the fact that they are immortal. In many ways animals are *more* spiritual than humans, but I'll get to that later. My closest spiritual connections to animals, like for many people, have been with dogs and cats. These are the pets that tend to share our everyday lives more closely. These are the ones that share our space and the first ones to greet us when we come home.

But anyone who owns a pet of any kind and loves it knows the terrible trauma that accompanies losing a companion that has often been with them on a day-to-day basis. We can sometimes miss them even more than people. We feel totally safe to tell our beloved pets anything. We feel they accept and understand us, and are with us in body and spirit through all the tough and all the happy moments of our lives, but also every ordinary moment in between. They're our constant companions and confidantes, and never tire of our company. They are never bored with us. Sometimes losing a companion such as this is, can be just as bad or even worse than losing a person, because pets give us a type of unconditional love that's unmatched in the world. In fact, even an animal that's been abused by its owner all its life will often still look upon that person with love and devotion.

My dog KC, a black Springer-Labrador cross, has been with me not just through one life but through many lives in many different bodies.

My Journeys with Animals

The Bravest Duck

Of recent times there's been a lot of press about foxes. Some people see them as part of Nature and appreciate their beauty. Others see them as a threat, either to their livelihood or even their person. Some people want to protect them, others to eradicate them mercilessly. Some of these are people full of emotion but no sense. To kill another creature is sometimes necessary, but to enjoy that killing and treat it as sport is not. I accept all parts and all aspects of the fox's nature, as I can demonstrate in the following two tales.

We used to keep chickens and ducks for a while for their eggs, and occasionally we'd have a visit from a fox. One day, we were gone for several hours and we failed to see a hole in the netting before we went out. The fox got in and, yes, it killed or attacked every bird. For fun? No. It was for survival.

We took the blame for the birds' deaths because, the way I see it quite honestly, we had built a 'fast food restaurant' in the middle of the foxes' territory (by setting up a chicken coop), so we couldn't really blame the foxes for wanting to sample the fare. I always felt it was up to us to keep the birds safe. We were very upset naturally to see the coop empty of life and the dead birds laid out in a line next to the hole in the fence. But the birds were dead, so we left them and the fox came back repeatedly and collected them one at a time, taking them off to stock his larder. The only reason foxes appear to kill everything and then abandon the bodies is because they've been disturbed, which gives rise to the myth that they kill for fun. Left alone, they won't waste a single death.

I said the fox killed them all, but we did in fact find one duck alive. She'd been bitten through the neck, though, and although the vet was able to save her life he couldn't do anything about the nerve damage she'd sustained. We thought about having her humanely destroyed, but after watching her for a while we couldn't bring ourselves to have this done. You see, that duck showed more courage and determination than any animal I'd ever seen. She would try to walk and the nerve damage in her neck would cause her to tumble over backwards. Undaunted, she'd get to her feet and try again, and again, never ever giving up. How could we not give her a chance? Miraculously she gradually became able to keep her balance for longer and longer, and a few weeks later she had just a slight twist in her neck to show for her ordeal. She taught me a lot about persistence and perseverance, and I never hated the fox, for it had no cruel intent.

Saving Mr Fox

When we moved home in Somerset a few years ago, we made sure we weren't smack bang in the middle of a hunt's territory. All around us was land where hunting wasn't allowed, either with gun or dog, so we weren't going to witness any atrocities – or so I thought.

One Tuesday afternoon I was sitting in the conservatory thinking how funny it was that all the pheasants in the area seemed to congregate in our garden. My hubby, Tony, always reckoned I called them in. We could hear guns, but only off in the far distance, and the birds would have been perfectly safe anywhere in the village. But every day they came, dozens of them, male and female. Tony said that they were attracted by my thought waves, knowing they'd be safe near me. Maybe he was right because it wasn't long before a peacock in full regalia also turned up, and then, incredibly, a pair of moorhens, even though we had no water in the garden!

Anyway, back to that Tuesday. In the distance I could hear a strange sound, and we suspected after a while that it was a hunting horn. We couldn't see any horses or riders, though, and we're quite high up so we figured they were miles away. The huntsmen might have been, but it turned out their hounds weren't. Hunts nowadays follow trails, as hunting has, quite rightly, been banned, but hounds don't always follow the right scent, and can stray onto a 'live' one. They are notoriously hard to control once they hit a scent, and hunts can't always get them back on track. This is why I feel the law needs to be tightened up.

The first sign that there'd be trouble came when I heard the distinct telepathic voice of a fox in severe distress. It was literally screaming out in terror. I stood up.

'What?' asked Tony.

'It's a fox – they've got a fox…' I answered. 'Come on!'

I dashed outside, followed by Tony. We couldn't see anything. Then we heard hounds baying, coming closer.

I cried out to the fox in my mind, 'Come here boy, come on.' I could sense it was a male, a big dog fox. 'He's coming!' I yelled, legging it down our garden, which spanned about an acre. Tony followed.

Within a minute the fox popped out of the hedgerow and stood, panting, in front of us. I looked over the far side to a thick shrub. The fox got the message and ran that way, climbing up into the shrub.

Within another minute about 20 hounds poured into the garden. Heads down, oblivious to us, they started to track across the garden towards the shrub. Hounds are big dogs, and 20 is a lot of dogs of any size. I planted myself between them and the fox. There was no way we could really physically stop them. There were too many, and they were so focused on their prey that whatever we did they would have taken no notice of us.

At any second they'd find the fox and tear him to bits. There was only one thing for it. I closed my eyes and thought myself into the hounds' minds. I pictured them going back the way they'd come. My mind ached with the pressure of it, and then I suddenly felt a switch in their collective pack mind and opened my eyes. They were streaming away, back through the hedge and into the adjacent land. We weren't out of the woods yet, though. I had to keep concentrating, removing the scent of fox from our hedge. This went on for about 40 minutes, the hounds milling around next door, mystified as to where their quarry had gone.

Finally, just when I was getting exhausted, we heard the sound of a rapidly trotting horse going up the road. It was obviously a huntsman searching for his hounds because he was blowing his horn like mad. The hounds finally broke off their search and obeyed the call. It was 10 minutes before Mr Fox was brave enough to leave his cover and slink away. He spared us a glance of thanks as he went on his way.

The 'Secret World' Fox

During my time at Taunton TV as a presenter, one of my greatest pleasures was when we filmed live at the Secret World Wildlife Rescue Centre. One visit involved me being inside the fox enclosure. There were about six foxes in there, some that had been handed over by misguided people who had tried to keep them as pets, and some that had been found injured and nursed back to health but were not fit enough to be returned to the wild. Within minutes of my sitting down in the enclosure the foxes swarmed over me, and one female spent many minutes scenting me by rubbing her head over mine. I was told by the keeper that this meant she was making me a part of her family. I was incredibly honoured to be accepted in this way, and a video clip of the event can be seen on my website. During my filming with Secret World I also experienced a barn owl sitting on my shoulder, a bat squirming around in the warmth inside my sweater and being literally covered from head to foot in ferrets!

Ashley Peacock

When a peacock arrived in our garden out of the blue one day, we were suitably impressed with his beauty. It wasn't until quite recently when someone remarked how strange it was that we realized there was more going on than meets the eye. The peacock represents some of the most admired human characteristics and those that most of us would aspire to. An accepted symbol of integrity, its beauty shows us what we, too, can achieve when we have the courage to stick to our guns and show our true colours. In other cultures the peacock symbolizes nobility, honour, guidance, protection and alertness.

As I said, this peacock just turned up in the garden one day. He gradually became tamer as he got to know both us and KC, who understood very quickly that he wasn't considered an intruder and shouldn't be harassed by her. We soon named him 'Ashley', after

Ashley Peacock in the UK soap opera, Coronation Street, and he must have approved because he readily answers to that name. While he spends a lot of time in our garden, he is also a free spirit able to leave at any time, and this was an important part of the message he was bringing. I write regularly for magazines and my columns bring with them a certain amount of pressure (timescales and deadlines) as well as great responsibility. I've often noticed that psychics of all kinds who appear on TV are under extraordinary pressure to perform and, having worked in live TV for two years myself, I understand the timescales and commercialism of the media. It must be difficult to force things sometimes, to perform 'to order', for time is money on TV. I feel this peacock is a reminder to me that I must maintain my integrity at all times, and that any modest abilities I may have could vanish just as quickly as they seemed to arrive. Like the legend of the ravens at the Tower of London, should the peacock ever desert me I would know that my downfall would have been of my own making. I have been warned!

I had to add something to this chapter today. We'd been having some building work done and, as is usual when there's any disturbance going on at the house, Ashley disappeared off elsewhere. The problem was that a week later we still hadn't seen or heard from him. Usually, even if he's not in our garden, we can hear him 'hooting' in the distance, but not this time. As he is a free spirit we have no say over where he chooses to go, whether he gets across the road safely or whether a predator, animal or human, might harm him, so we got increasingly worried as the days went by and there was no sign. Then I woke up at 4 a.m. this morning because I was so concerned, and I lay there brooding over his possible fate and how to discover it. We'd already driven up and down the lane to make sure he wasn't lying injured on the road somewhere, but, like anyone when the 'night nadgers' strike, I became very down about it. Then I thought, why didn't I talk to him? And I started to call to him in my mind, asking could he please give us a sign that he was all right – or, indeed, let us know if he was not. My restlessness woke Tony up, too, and at 5 a.m. he got up, only to immediately call back to me from the kitchen, 'Ashley's out on the patio!' I was so relieved! He has stayed with us all day, carefully watching the building progress and examining the workers' lunch at midday, and then he glided away, his long tail sweeping the ground like a bride's train. This time I won't worry if he doesn't come back while the work's going on, because I know that he can 'hear' me.

Feeding the Swans

When I was still quite small, I scared Mum with my apparent casual attitude to animals. We used to visit Southsea, in Hampshire, for holidays at my Aunt May's hotel. What I used to like best was feeding the seagulls as they soared overhead. I soon learned that if I threw the bread as high as I could, one of these supreme flying acrobats would snatch it out of the air before it could fall to Earth. I really admired their peerless ability in the air. One particular day Mum took me to the park and I happily wandered around while she sat on a bench. The next thing she knew, I was surrounded by about seven swans. Unbeknown to Mum I'd had half a loaf in my pocket and had decided to offer it to these really big 'seagulls'. Mum said the swans were taller than me, and she really didn't know what to do as I stood in the middle of a circle of huge white birds, with their flashing beaks and flapping wings. As she rushed over, though, she realized to her amazement that I had the situation totally under control. I was giving each bird in turn a piece of bread, scolding any that tried to grab an extra crumb, pushing any greedy beaks aside, and the swans, amazingly, were being really gentle with me. When all the bread was gone I just told them all to go away, and they did.

Monkey Business

Another event demonstrating my strong connection with animals happened with my brother's monkey. My brother was the only other person in the family who had a strong desire to own a pet. But he only wanted a monkey, so that might have been more to do with the kudos of having an exotic pet rather than loving animals in general. The monkey's name showed no originality at all: Cheetah, after the chimp by the same name in the Tarzan films. I don't know what type of monkey Cheetah was, as I was only about eight years old at the time, but he looked like a small chimpanzee. He had a large pen in the garden and was a little difficult to handle, often nipping people. Mum told me that one day she looked out of the window to see me walking round the garden with Cheetah slung on my hip, his arms around me, much in the way a mother might carry a toddler. I can even remember the feeling of doing it, with the monkey's warm little body clamped to mine. I had no fear at all. Cheetah was re-homed to a zoo not long after that, where he was able to live with others of his kind, partly because I kept saying it should be so, and also because he clearly wasn't happy in his cage, which was why he nipped people.

An Injured Bird

I became a real tomboy, and my childhood memories are of endless, hazy, sunny days spent outdoors in the company of animals as much as possible. But my rapport with animals, and my compassion for them, soon became a bit of a burden to me because the slightest hurt suffered by any helpless creature, human or animal, was like a deep wound to me. I distinctly remember the day I realized I was different from the rest of my family. We were on the way to the shops in the car when we came upon a bird – it was a red-legged partridge – just sitting in the middle of the road, not even trying to run away from the approaching car, let alone fly. 'Stop the car!' I yelled. My dad did stop the car, but he wasn't best pleased. 'There's nothing you can do,' he told me, with a hint of impatience.

I got out of the car and approached the bird. It staggered as if drunk, and I cupped my hands around it and lifted it up. It had no marks or injuries on it, and its wings and legs were undamaged, but it had obviously been struck a glancing blow by a car, which had stunned it. I took it over to the side of the road, straddled the wire fence and carefully placed it in the undergrowth, where it could take its time to recover in safety. I was certain it would soon be back to normal.

To me this bird was everything to do with us, whereas to my family it was of no concern, and I was just being 'silly'. I puzzled over this for years. How could one person be totally unable to leave an injured creature to fend for itself, whereas other people could walk away without a thought? I almost fell out with various members of my family on many issues relating to what they did and what went on in their homes over the years – holes in fascia boards they would fill in to stop house-martins nesting inside sheds, bats that were crushed to death because they had invaded a bedroom by accident, a cat my Dad left for dead after he'd hit it with his car, without checking if it was still alive or informing its owners, who might have spent months searching for their pet. I'd get furious – but don't get me wrong, my family aren't deliberately cruel or heartless people. They are good people, but they just didn't connect with animals at all, whereas I loved animals more than I loved most people.

Sedona, Arizona

Despite the concern it can cause your family, it can be very useful to have a strong rapport with the animal kingdom because, if you're lucky, you can access their wisdom and knowledge and use their strong instincts when yours may have failed. Something that happened while Tony and I were visiting the stunning town of Sedona, in Arizona, proved this to me.

Sedona is an oasis of green in the middle of the hot, dusty Arizona countryside. It's surrounded by the most beautiful, wind-sculpted red rocks, all of which have names inspired by their shapes: Cathedral, Bell, Castle and Kachina Woman among them. There are also four powerful energy vortexes in the area, each one near a different red rock.

We wanted to get up close to Kachina Woman, which you can't see from the road as it's hidden by a knoll. It's quite a difficult walk without a guide, as the trail is not at all clear. We set off from the nearest carpark and soon became quite lost. The temperature was 100°F (nearly 38°C), and Arizona has rattlesnakes as well as scorpions, black widow spiders and tarantulas, among others, so we were a little nervous. Before long we realized we'd been right to be nervous because we were hopelessly lost.

Every bush and patch of sandy soil looked the same, and soon we had no idea where the rock was or, more worryingly, which way would lead us back to our car. The sun beat down on our heads and we tried not to panic as we started to feel very vulnerable.

Suddenly, a small blue bird appeared on the ground in front of us. He cocked his head as if to say hello, and then hopped along between two trees. Then he came back to us and repeated the same actions. *Follow me*, I heard. Realizing he was there to help, we followed him. He hopped along and cocked his head repeatedly as if to make sure we were following, and before long we came to the Kachina Woman Rock. We were very relieved, and the bird disappeared as suddenly as he'd come. We stood and meditated in the vortex field of the rock, and the messages were wonderful, assuring us that things were going to work out. As the energy swept through us, we felt transported back to an era when the Earth was worshipped and venerated and the area was peopled with noble races who should never have been driven out.

When the time came to leave, we had no idea how to find our way back to the car, but I called out with my mind to the little bird, who once again appeared and led us back to the part of the track that was well-worn enough to follow.

Close Encounters with Big Cats

For my 30th birthday Tony organized a rather special and unique surprise, which was to test my fearlessness and connection with animals in a wondrous and magical way. He wouldn't tell me where we were going until the actual day of the surprise, and even then all I knew was that we were going to Colchester Zoo, our local zoo at the time, which was renowned for its conservation programmes. Tony knew a secret desire I had. I was pretty obsessed with big cats, and ever since I was a child I'd wanted to get up close to some and try and communicate with them.

When we got to the zoo I was approached by a keeper and the surprise was revealed. I was to accompany him on his rounds and would be able to feed all the big cats. I was stunned. Any distaste I might have had for handling hunks of raw meat was totally eclipsed by the thrill of close contact with the cats. I was pretty amazed that the zoo was willing to let someone like me get so close to the wild animals. Even today, the more I think about it, the more bizarre it seems.

They started me off with the jackals, which I took to be a bit of a test – of my trust in the keeper, of my ability to follow his instructions and of my nerve. I was sent in alone, a joint of meat in each hand, and told to crouch down, holding them at arm's length. The keeper told me the jackals would growl and snarl and run around me, but they wouldn't touch me and I must show no fear. I could sense as they ran around me, growling, that they were afraid of me and just wanted their food, despite their bravado. After a few minutes they plucked up the courage to snatch the meat and run off with it. Next, I graduated up to a hyena, which was a bit bigger and a bit fiercer. I was told that, so long as I showed no fear, I would be safe. I felt no fear at all, as I could sense with all of these animals that all they were concerned about was getting fed.

After that it got really exciting, as in turn I fed a cheetah, a black panther and the jaguars. Each of these were ordered (by me) to go into their 'houses', which they did, while I placed the meat strategically in their pens, and then released them again. Word seemed to get round because, as after a while, as soon as I approached the next pen the cats would immediately go into their houses without being told – well, not in words anyway.

The tigers and lions were an eye-opener, as this was the first time I'd ever been up close to one, and they were a lot bigger than they looked from a distance. In the case of the lions, the procedure was a bit different. I went with the keeper behind the glass screen that separates the inner cages from the public. Then I was told to stick my hand, clutching a joint of meat, through a small panel in their cage wall, while the lions watched from their outdoor pen. The keeper held on to my arm because, he told me, the lions would come in extremely fast, and if I didn't pull my hand back in time, they were quite capable of getting their paw through the hole and ripping my arm off.

The male lion stunned me with the speed at which he leapt almost 4 metres (12 feet) from a standing start, landing right inside the cage. In a spilt second he'd grabbed the meat, as the keeper, with perfect timing, deftly whipped my hand away.

After that came what was the most thrilling part of the day for me. I was taken to the snow leopard's pen. These cats are incredibly beautiful, with their striking markings. I was instructed to go inside the safety pen and shut the door behind me before opening the door into his proper pen, where the snow leopard was lying on the ground, about 3 metres (10 feet) from the door, waiting and watching. Were they really going to let me go into this cat's presence, unarmed, undefended and alone? Yes, they were. I'll never understand why I was allowed to do this. Even if the cat had been hand-reared, all big cats are still wild animals and have been known to turn on their keepers in a flash; and even if the zoo carried public liability insurance, can you imagine any insurance company paying out in these circumstances? Public liability doesn't cover the risk of allowing a member of the public into a cage with a big cat!

Anyway, I was then told to go into the pen, holding the meat in front of me, and approach the cat, keeping full eye contact at all times. Then I was to place the meat about a metre in front of him and back out, still keeping eye contact. My heart was pounding with joy as I walked towards the snow leopard where he lay, and our eyes connected. I felt not a flicker of fear. The cat's eyes spoke to me, telling me I was quite safe, as I leaned down to place the meat at his feet. The absolute thrill of being so close to such a gorgeous wild animal, with no barrier between us, overrode every other emotion. I felt so privileged. This was probably the most 'in the moment' I'd ever been. It was a day I'll never forget.

Beachcombing

All through the years, my bond with animals has remained strong, and a major factor in my life. Once, Tony and I were walking along the beach in Great Yarmouth, in Norfolk, when we noticed some sort of fuss going on a little way ahead of us. As we reached the spot we saw that several young lads were standing in a circle, looking at something on the ground. Being curious, we stopped to see what was going on. A shag (a bird like a cormorant) was standing on the sand. The boys were throwing it bits of bacon, which it was gobbling down greedily. That was nice of them. The awful thing was that the bird was covered in oil. In that state it could neither swim, fly nor preen its feathers, and it certainly couldn't get any more food or, more importantly, water for itself. The boys told us they'd been keeping it alive for two days by feeding it scraps. I asked why they hadn't taken it to a rescue centre, because apart from anything else it would soon succumb to hypothermia with the oil all over it. They replied that they didn't like to try and pick it up in case it bit them. It *was* a fearsome-looking bird, it's true, about the size of a goose with a large, curved beak, and I didn't blame them for being wary, but the shag cried out to me for help.

I looked at Tony, and with a 'here we go again' expression on his face he watched me walk up to the bird, pick it up and tuck it under my arm. I wasn't being brave. I knew it wouldn't bite because it had told me so, just as it had told me it wouldn't run or struggle. We took it to the Coast Guard Station, and they phoned for a rescue centre to come and get it. At least the boys had cared, even if they hadn't really known the best thing to do!

We love to feed the birds here at our current home in Somerset, and we've counted over 30 species that visit our bird table. Occasionally, a bird flies into our windows, despite the stickers all over them, and falls to the ground, stunned. Each and every one is collected and put inside a warm box next to the oven to recover before being released. Left cold and still on the concrete, they'd soon die of shock or hypothermia, or become prey to a predator.

Encounters with Deer

Another time I got a message through animals was when we were walking KC, our dog, on the Quantock Hills. Tony was waiting for some quite serious hospital test results at the time, and I was hoping for some sort of sign that would help me feel secure about them. The Quantocks are an amazing spiritual place, and the energy is fantastic there. We were strolling along when some sixth sense made me turn around. I grabbed Tony's arm and turned him around, too. Filing past us, at a canter, was a whole herd of about 30 red deer. They were totally silent as they poured past, so silent that KC didn't even hear or see them, and she continued sniffing around in the grass as they passed us. The other strange thing, apart from their silent passage, was that, after they'd gone over the hill, we ran to the top (just a few yards) to watch them go and there was no sign of them, no deer in sight and not a single mark in the heather or gorse to mark their passing. I took this to be a good sign about the test results, and so it proved to be.

Just the other day, I was driving home up a steep hill. This road is full of sharp bends as well as being uphill all the way, so the tendency is to have your foot on the accelerator as much as possible, otherwise there's a chance your car won't make it. As usual I was rolling along taking the bends as fast as was safe, when suddenly I 'heard' the words, *I'm here, slow down.* I immediately slowed down to a crawl round the final bend, which was totally blind, and there, standing in the middle of the road, was a beautiful female roe deer.

If I'd been going any faster I'd have been unable to avoid hitting her, which would have been something I'd never have recovered from, I'm sure. I braked and stopped, and she didn't move at first, obviously unafraid, and our eyes met briefly through the windscreen of my car. I had time to admire her beautiful chestnut coat and her big black eyes, and then she tip-toed daintily across the road and slipped into the hedge at the side, vanishing silently in a few seconds.

Communicating

As I reached my teens, while other girls were obsessed with boyfriends and makeup, I was roaming around, usually dressed in jodhpurs, usually pretty grubby and usually trying to rescue some animal or other. I was always bringing home waifs and strays and installing them in various boxes and cages while I tried to help them recover from whatever injuries had befallen them.

One pivotal time that I vividly recall, which made me understand why and how I had such a great connection to animals, was when a sparrow had flown into our glass back door and was lying on the ground, unable to move. I picked it up. The poor little thing's tail was cocked up at a very odd angle, like a wren's, and it was obviously in great distress. I held the bird gently in my hands, wondering what to do for the best. To my astonishment, I heard the words in my mind: *my tail, put my tail back*. Not really believing I could work a miracle, not sure if I'd really heard anything, and terrified of hurting the bird more, I nevertheless carefully manipulated the tail downwards, towards its correct position. Suddenly, with a satisfying 'click', the tail popped back into its socket and was straight again. With total joy I opened my hands and the bird flew off, straight and true. I was ecstatic, and suddenly had the revelation that my connection to animals wasn't just some mysterious sort of rapport, they were actually communicating with me. It was just that, up till then, I'd been too young to understand the concept.

After that this communication started to happen on a regular basis. When I'd find injured animals, they'd be able to tell me what they needed. Most of them wanted a quiet, dark, warm place to rest, sometimes to recover, and some of them just wanted a private place to die in peace.

Sometimes it was very hard to hear animals' pleas and not be able to help as much as I'd have liked. One time, after Tony and I were married, we were driving along the motorway when, perched right on the white line that divided the slow lane from the hard shoulder, there was a cat. It wasn't close to death, and it was sitting up, but it was obviously injured and unable to move, and equally obviously terrified. *Help me!* I heard in my mind. All this I saw and heard in a spilt second, as we flashed past. But by the time my mind had recognized what I'd seen and heard in that spilt second, we were already several hundred yards down the road, and the traffic was moving nose-to-tail and very fast. Stopping quickly wasn't an option. Anyway, stopping on the motorway, even on the hard shoulder, unless broken down, was very dangerous and certainly illegal. Even as I thought about what to do for the best we were travelling at speed ever further away. Then I saw a motorway phone ahead.

Tony pulled over, hazard lights flashing. I opened the little door of the emergency phone booth, pulled out the phone and dialled the number, conscious of the stream of traffic thundering by, much too close for comfort. This only made me even more aware of what that poor cat was going through, as it was much closer to the carriageway than I was. The man who answered the phone didn't seem to think an injured cat was much of an emergency. It was for the *cat*, I told him. In the end I had to tell him the animal was causing a hazard, that cars were swerving round it, and that there was bound to be a big accident, which would be his fault if he did nothing. He agreed to send out an emergency vehicle to pick up the cat. All day I reached out intuitively, hoping to hear more from the cat, but there was nothing. I thought perhaps it had died before it could be helped, or perhaps we were too far away by then for it to reach me. I gave up, but then on the way home we passed that spot again, and of course I looked across the carriageways and thought of the cat, picturing it in my mind. All of a sudden I could sense the flash of relief that the cat had felt as it had been picked up, so I knew it had been taken to help.

Empathy with Animals

The empathy I feel with animals has made life very difficult at times, and as I have grown and forged my own spiritual path, I still have daily problems coping with the feelings I get. Seeing people ill-treating a defenceless animal makes my blood boil. If I see a dog locked in a car on a hot day, I can't walk away, because the dog will call out to me to help it. Many times I've waited and confronted the owner when they've returned to their car, asking them to sit locked in it for a while themselves and see how they like it. Once or twice when they've been too long, I've phoned the police or RSPCA and had them break into the cars. One time the car wasn't locked and I was able to get a beautiful but very distressed Golden Retriever out, much to the surprise and anger of the owner when he returned from an outdoor bowls match. Luckily, I was able to convince him that I'd done the right thing, and eventually he thanked me for saving his dog.

When I see a container full of sheep, pigs or cattle on their way to the abattoir, I can feel their distress and confusion. They often know exactly where they're going, having picked up images from their handlers, so I sense their fear as well. The only help I can offer in that moment is to envision wrapping that lorry-load in the light and warmth of their creator and let them go with love. I'm sure that in a couple of hundred years man will look back on these times with the guilt he now feels over the way slaves were once kept and treated.

My Dogs

My very earliest memory of my first connection to an animal is a little fuzzy, because it took place when I was only two years old, but when I was older my mum filled in the gaps.

Sally

Although my family weren't really all that fussed about having animals in the house, they'd been persuaded to take on a two-year-old dog called Sally, a Bull Terrier-Boxer cross. She was very striking to look at, being smooth-haired, mostly black with just a white bib and ginger accessories like her eyebrows, bracelets on her legs and a thin ginger line dividing her white bib from the rest of her black coat. Mum had been assured she was a well-behaved, non-aggressive dog, but she didn't suspect just how thoroughly I was going to test that guarantee out!

On the day of her arrival, Sally was given a big marrowbone and let into the garden with it, where she soon settled down and started chewing contentedly. A few minutes later Mum was distracted by the arrival of a neighbour, and when she came back into the kitchen and looked out of the window, she saw, to her horror, her two-year-old toddler (me) tottering across the grass to the dog and bending down to grab the bone from her jaws. Not having time to do anything more than yell out of the window, which might have triggered a bad reaction from the dog, my mother could only watch in fear at what might happen next. Apparently, after I'd nonchalantly reached down and grabbed the bone, I walked off with it, with poor Sally following along behind me. That moment was the start of a lifelong friendship.

Because Sally was two and I was two when she came to the family, we grew up together. She was my constant escort and guardian. I remember my Uncle Phil, who was a very kindly soul, waving an arm around my head once as he tried to swat a fly away from me. Thinking he was going to hit me, Sally leapt between us and grabbed and held his arm. She didn't bite him – she never bit – but she held him tight all the same. From quite a young age I was completely safe to roam around the countryside, so long as I had my guardian, Sally, with me. She was my playmate and my best friend for 12 years, and we went everywhere together.

Tasha

Tasha was a Lhasa Apso, with long grey hair and was chosen as a puppy by our son when he was about three. She was a wonderful little dog, but she was a member of the family and not a dog that I connected with on a deep level.

Peri

Peri was a Jack Russell crossed with a collie, long haired, lemon and white. Again she was a dear little girl, and I loved her, but no really deep unity.

Snoopy

Snoopy was my little pal. He was such a fun little dog to be around. A rather ungainly shape, with short legs and a long body (must have been some dachshund in there somewhere!) He was black, smooth coated, with incredibly silky fur. People used to comment on it whenever they touched him. My fondest memories of him are from a holiday in Cornwall, where the cottage came with its own swimming pool. Sounds glamorous but actually the water was green and inhabited by frogs! Snoopy loved it though, he was a very loving and genuine little dog.

Nyssa

Such an adorable little pet. She too was black, smooth coated (yes there is a pattern developing here – all the dogs I ever had that were really close to me have been black with short hair!) I have no idea yet, why that might be. Nyssa stuck to me like glue. Like Snoopy she had been a rescue dog – something almost all my dogs have in common, too. When I picked her up at the rescue centre, she was in a pen of Springer Spaniels that were so much bigger and livelier than her that I almost didn't see her at first. I was just thinking they didn't have anyone for me, when I saw her peering out from the pack. Her facial expression when I picked her up and 'saved her from the horde' was priceless. I always said that Nyssa would never, ever bite anyone, or even growl at them, and it was true. She was the gentlest dog I ever knew.

Ace

Ace was a big black dog, and anyone who met her during her prime couldn't fail to be either impressed by her beauty or intimidated by her power, and which one of the two they perceived depended entirely on their intentions. She was normally a very gentle creature, even cleaning and nurturing any of our newborn lambs that were rejected by their mothers, but let anyone threaten to lay a hand on me or the rest of her 'pack' and she would change instantly into a tiger.

This image of her is a far cry from when she came to us. At that point she'd been a 13-week old, pathetic, scarred little bundle of insecurity. Her previous owner had burned her, leaving her chest and the top of one leg mostly hairless. At the time the rescue centre that had saved her were having trouble rehoming her. People didn't relish the thought of walking down the street with a scarred dog on a lead, worried perhaps that passers-by might think they were the ones who had inflicted the damage on her. Other kind people had tried to home her but found her too clingy, too desperate, too scared and basically too much trouble. I know now that she was waiting for me. None of her issues at that age worried us. From the moment this traumatized puppy walked the few paces from the rescue lady to sit quietly at my side like a much older dog, as if to say, 'Thank goodness, you've come at last,' she owned me, mind, body and soul.

There followed a few years when alternately she saved me from an enraged ram and an intruder, and I saved her from a rampaging swarm of wasps and a near-drowning in the local river. We came to trust one another implicitly. Throughout my journey to spiritual enlightenment, I've had many other personal incidents that have convinced me that animals not only have souls but, in some ways, some of them are more spiritual than we are. And the biggest impact any experience with animals has had on me was with Ace. She was the closest an animal soul could ever get to a human soul. She was my shadow, and I loved her almost more than life. I lived in dread of the time when something happened to her, because I knew I would be almost destroyed by grief, and the terrible need to know that she still existed somewhere, and was safe, would eat away at me. It's a cruel trick, having dogs not live as long as their masters.

Of course when it happened as it inevitably had to, and when Ace lay lifeless on our living room floor, I simply couldn't cope with the bottomless chasm her absence created in my heart. We didn't have much of a garden, and I didn't want to go to some anonymous disposal site, so we had her cremated. When I was handed a tin with her ashes in, my grief made me open it. I felt total disbelief that the little fragments the tin contained were all that was left of my gorgeous, lion-hearted dog. It just was impossible to believe, and I didn't believe it – she was still out there, somewhere. Her indomitable soul had to still exist. This was a defining moment for me because while I'd always believed our pets had to live on, this was the first time that I held in my hands the proof. For no one will ever convince me that a being so wonderful could ever just be snuffed out.

I feel that sometimes the depth of our grief can 'block' a spirit, human or animal, from getting through to us. I think this is why manifestations or communications from those we have lost often don't come through for some time, perhaps not until after the grief has dulled a little.

For six months I grieved constantly, crying at some point every day, sobbing when my hand reached for what had been her constant presence, only to find empty space. She had always been next to me, at any hour. Even when she'd grown too old to really see me, her faithful sense of smell would enable her to sense my movements and follow them. I used to get up sneakily, hoping to leave her for a moment sleeping, not wanting her to struggle onto her stiff legs just to accompany me into the kitchen for a moment, but it never worked. I could not fool her.

No more, I vowed. I would never have another dog. For one thing, I didn't want any other dog that wasn't her. And I knew that I couldn't stand another loss like that one. It was better, I thought, to not love and therefore not lose.

I was wrong. We can never have too much love in our world, despite the pain it can bring. Like most owners I felt that I would never 'betray her memory' by trying to replace her, but it turned out I didn't have to.

Dogless, and therefore free (I had never liked having to go away and leave Ace during her whole life, and had rarely done it), Tony and I went to Arizona, to the beautiful and mystical town of Sedona, for our first holiday in years. It was a magical place, surrounded by huge red rocks, a green oasis in the desert. There, I had a psychic reading, six months after Ace had died, on 13 September, during which the medium, unasked, tapped into 'a big black dog with grey whiskers'. I was told that this dog was 'a spark of my soul', and with this information came a sort of epiphany. I came to understand one of the great truths. When pets are so connected that the relationship between them and their owner almost transcends that of two humans, and when the understanding between the two is so remarkable that it verges on telepathic, then those pets are sparks, part of their owner's soul. The comfort in this, and what I felt instantly, is that these two can never really be parted. I was also told, 'Today I am young again'. At the time I assumed she meant she was in heaven, healed of all her age-related pains.

Some people have spoken to me of a feeling of being hit in the chest, sometime after their pet has passed, and that the gentle blow lifts them out of their spiralling depression following the loss of their companion. This 'blow' is the feeling they get when the spark of their soul, the one that resided in their pet, comes back to them. It's a reunion on a spiritual level and completes the person once again. No wonder the pain of one of these pets passing is so dire and deep. No wonder a person in that position feels as if part of them is missing, for it is exactly that.

Despite all my experience and the little messages I got from Ace, I needed another psychic person to bring me her most important message. When we were back home we had our attention drawn to a litter of 'springadors' (Springer Spaniels crossed with Labradors) which had been born on the very same day that I'd had the reading in Arizona. When we went to see them, a feeling of déjà vu stole over us as one strangely quiet puppy behaved towards me in exactly the same way as Ace had when we'd first met her. When the puppy turned over in my arms and displayed her pink tummy, we could see that she had been born with a nipple missing – the same nipple Ace had lost in surgery a few years before she'd died. That wasn't the end of the story, either. A few weeks later I received a drawing from psychic artist June-Elleni Laine, which she said had come to her from a black German shepherd cross Labrador, which was exactly the breed Ace had been, with the message, 'This is me.' The drawing was an exact portrayal, in every detail, of the new puppy we'd called KC. Ace had returned to us in a new body.

As well as sharing important physical feature with Ace, there are many things KC just seems to know, from having been Ace in her previous life. For instance, one common area for accidents with any small animal under your feet is when you're carrying a container of anything hot. The chances of tripping over your pet are high. But Ace was badly scalded as a puppy (by her previous owners) with a kettle full of hot water, and KC will immediately get well out of the way, without being told, as soon as you pick up any container of anything hot, including a kettle, of which she's particularly wary.

KC also gave me one quite amusing sign that she was indeed Ace returned. In our garden we had a beautiful little rose tree that I planted over Ace's ashes. After blooming abundantly for several months, the rose tree suddenly died for no apparent reason. I was a bit upset, and left it in place for some time, hoping it would recover. After a while I saw the reason for the rose's demise. KC was urinating on it! This was out of character as KC is normally very well-behaved in the garden, never digs up plants and is always very circumspect in her toilet habits, always finding secluded and accepted areas to 'do her business'. At first, for a second, I was a bit annoyed, but then I was joyful again. KC was showing me that there was no need for a memorial to her previous self. She was back!

My Cats

We've had many cats of our own, over the years.

Felix

Felix, our dear old long-haired black boy, lived until he was 17 years old. He was known as our talking cat, because he could meow in ways that sounded just like words, his most common being 'Hello', when we came home from somewhere. He would also use this 'word' when walking around the house on the outside and looking for someone to let him in.

Windy

Windy came to us during the famous 1987 hurricane, blown in from goodness knows where, as a kitten aged approximately eight weeks. We never did find out where she came from. She was a pretty washed-out, stripy grey cat. I was very close to her.

Rupert and Benji

Rupert and Benji were brothers of mixed fortunes. Found starving in a dog's bowl at five weeks old, they had to be hand-reared under vet supervision. Sadly, Rupert was killed by a speeding car in our very quiet lane as soon as he became full-grown and beautiful.

However, Benji lived to a ripe old age and was more of a dog-parrot than a cat really, as he would come to call, like a speeding rocket, and run right up my body and onto my shoulder. I was really attached to this cat, but I never had any really mystical experiences with him, apart from when Benji and our family parted company, with his blessing.

My Horses

The Pony with Homing Instinct

When I was young I longed to own my own pony, but it wasn't to happen until I was in my twenties. However, children and animals have a special bond if they love each other, and I wasn't short on opportunities to learn this. My dad knew a man who lived about 10 miles from us. He was a rough diamond, someone who dealt in scrap metal, and he always had a pony or two around the place. He let me ride a little pony of his called Jigsaw. He was very pretty, a blue roan, quite small but very strong and effervescent. I loved him, and we certainly bonded, but I'd only been going to ride him for a couple of weeks when his owner rang with some sad news: Jigsaw had broken out of his paddock and vanished. It was very odd that a pony would run away from its secure home, but it seemed as if he had.

I persuaded my dad to drive me around in the car near to where Jigsaw lived in the hope that we'd come across him, but we didn't. The police were informed but nobody came forward to say they'd found him. It was a mystery. A few days later I was out walking and passed by a yard behind a café, about half a mile from where I lived. Through the open gateway I could see two men trying to corner a pony. I couldn't believe my eyes: it was Jigsaw! The men saw me looking and called out to ask if I knew of anyone who'd lost a pony. Even they couldn't believe it when I told them the pony had come from the town 10 miles away. To get to this place he'd had to cross two major roads and make his way through acres of woodland and farms. The fact that he'd ended up in my backyard, so to speak, and without anyone seeing him, was really odd. Although he'd been acting wild with the men who were trying to catch him, he calmed immediately I walked up to him and tamely allowed me to put a halter on him. Why did he run away? How did he end up there? Had he been trying to find me? I really think he had.

Sky's the Limit

I also had an incredible, 20-year relationship with my Welsh cob horse, Sky. He was a very beautiful boy, of that there's no doubt, but he wasn't really what would be considered ideal, or natural, eventing material. Because of the speed, stamina and jumping ability required in the cross-country element, event horses are generally at least three-quarter thoroughbred – that is, bred to race.

Being a Welsh cob, Sky was stocky, with high knee action (which slowed him down), a chunky body and a lack of stamina. Nevertheless he had a huge heart and, most important of all, we understood each other. Despite all the odds, Sky scooted round the cross-country element of the events in a courageous and determined way, beating all the aristocratic thoroughbred horses on more than one occasion. His achievements amazed everyone, especially his competitors, and a lot of that was due to the fact that most of them were constantly misunderstanding what their horses were trying to tell them, whereas Sky and I were in constant communication. He was one in a million, and he taught me what a person and an animal together can achieve when they're a true team.

CHAPTER 1

All about Dogs

There's a lot more to dogs than meets the eye. It's very easy for some people to dismiss animals as 'stupid', but I'm always sad when this happens because it means that many dogs out there are not being allowed to fulfil their real potential! Look at it differently, and you'll see that in many ways dogs prove themselves to be more than mere 'animals' in so many ways.

What Are Dreams?

Conventionally, dreams are the brain's way of processing the events of the day, so that your mind can categorize what is useful and what is not, give you ways to resolve issues that weren't sorted out during the day and allow you to re-live difficult or pleasurable moments from the day's activities. But there is a short period at the start and end of normal deep sleep during which very odd things can happen. It is said that in these transitional moments we have access to other realms and spiritual guidance, and that important messages can come through from angels, from the universe, from loved ones who have passed over and even from our own past lives. As a human you can confirm or deny that you know this happens, because you have the power of speech. Most people, when they think about it, have experienced that time just as sleep overcomes the brain, or that waking moment just before they return to full consciousness, when 'dreams' change into something quite different and infinitely mystical.

Do Dogs Dream?

But can this possibly apply to dogs? First of all, dogs – and in fact all animals except those that go into deep hibernation – remain responsive to stimuli in everything but the deepest REM (rapid eye movement) sleep. So, they are often in the state described above when literally 'half asleep'. We've all seen our dogs twitch, jerk their legs as if running or swimming and make noises from growls to little barks, while asleep, so there can be no doubt in anyone's mind that our dogs do dream. But if you take the definition of dreaming as outlined above, then dogs certainly do more than just dream in order to review the day's events. Our dog, KC, for instance, will often 'suckle' in her sleep – the noise and tongue movements are unmistakable – and yet she has not suckled now for many years, so this is a distant memory, not one from the day on which she is dreaming about it. She will sometimes 'run' and growl ferociously when asleep, in a way we have never seen her do when awake, which would suggest this could be a memory from a past life, perhaps lived as a wolf. Next time you see your dog dreaming, try to figure out what that dream might be about, and you could discover a whole new side to him.

Magical Dogs

Dogs and humans have been connected for thousands of years and many cultures have strange beliefs about dogs. The Native American Ojibwa tribe tell that the first dogs came to Earth from another realm. Legend says that once a group of Ojibwas were blown off course in their canoe onto a strange beach. There they met a friendly giant, but also an evil spirit called a *windigo*, which wanted to eat them. They became afraid but were saved by what they thought was a monster: a creature that the giant called a dog. The dog killed the *windigo* and the Ojibwas were then taken safely home by the dog, which left them near their village and then disappeared. For some time the rest of the tribe didn't believe in the existence of the dog but eventually it returned and it stayed with them.

Norwegians have another version of how they came to invite dogs into their lives. They say that a long time ago some humans were trying to herd reindeer, but the more they ran around and shouted, the more the reindeer scattered. Two dogs were watching their attempts and decided that they could do better, so they ran down and quickly drove the reindeer into a circle. The men were so grateful that they formed a partnership with the dogs.

Other legends about dogs include:

Gelert: A legendary dog associated with the village of Beddgelert (meaning Gelert's Grave) in Gwynedd, northwest Wales. The dog belonged to Llewellyn the Great, Prince of Gwynedd, and was a gift from King John of England. One day Llewellyn returned from hunting to find his baby's cradle overturned, the baby missing and the dog with blood around its mouth. Imagining the worst, Llewellyn killed the dog with his sword. But then he heard the baby crying and found it hidden under the cradle, next to the dead body of a wolf. Devastated at his mistake, Llewellyn buried the dog with great ceremony, but after that day he never smiled again.

Maera: In Greek mythology this was the hound of Erigone, who was the daughter of Icarius, who had been taught how to make wine. Icarius was a follower of the wine god Dionysus. One day Icarius was killed by a band of shepherds. When her father failed to return home Erigone was worried, so she took her dog and went to look for him. Maera led her to his grave, and both of them were overwhelmed with grief: Erigone hanged herself and Maera leaped off a cliff. The god Dionysus then placed them in the sky and they became the constellation of Virgo and the star Procyon.

Do Dogs Have Angels?

If you believe that people have angels, then you have to accept that perhaps dogs have angels, too. Some of the stories that are sent to me seem to suggest that dogs can become divine beings, sometimes for a while and sometimes for the whole of their lives, while some people believe that dogs can and do become angels.

If you think your dog was guided into your life, perhaps by an angel, think carefully about how your life has changed since you got him. Have your finances or prospects improved? Did you suddenly find a partner and embark on a wonderful relationship? If so, what part did your dog play in these events?

You may also have been led to your dog by a series of synchronistic events, or maybe you entered your dog's life, nudged there by a series of angel-inspired messages? There is a reason for everything and you and your dog coming together is no exception. Try making a list of the things in your life that have been affected by your dog or the things in his life that have been changed by you.

Your Dog's Mind

One of the reasons people give for not believing that animals are more than just beasts that happen to share the planet with us and are there for us to use as we will, is that they're not intelligent like us. This archaic view is sadly still held by too many. Recent research has shown that this is not the case. It is true that dogs would not make highly intelligent people, but then people would not make highly intelligent dogs either! According to test results the most intelligent dogs are border collies, who can understand a new command in five or fewer repetitions. So why not devote some time to stimulating your dog's intelligence and, in so doing, also increase his enjoyment of life.

Don't make the mistake of confusing intelligence with inbred behavioural characteristics. For instance, if you have a Labrador, he will instinctively retrieve items. If you have a collie, he will naturally herd. True intelligence is gauged by the dog's ability to find solutions to problems, and to act in a way that shows an awareness of consequences. For instance, one way KC shows her intelligence is when and where to do her business if we're going out. She knows the difference between when we are say we are going for a 'long' time or we will be 'quick', and she takes that into consideration. So far she has always made the right choice. This demonstrates an element of self-awareness and reasoning as to possible consequences of her decisions – a sure sign of conventionally accepted intelligence. Try getting some of the excellent interactive dog games that are available now for your dog: you might well be astonished at what he can do.

How You and Your Dog Can Help Others

Your Dog's Personal Development

Every single creature on the Earth, including us, has come here to learn and progress. We all need to feel, even if subconsciously, that we're developing, otherwise there's little point in us being here. The same can be said of your dog. Every dog, from those with apparently little intelligence, to those that seem almost human in their understanding and reasoning powers, needs to learn, so that he can eventually return to spirit, changed for the better. Dogs are very adept learners because of their innate need to please their owners, and by teaching them, you'll also be nurturing their need to improve.

Having a Dog Can Change Things

Dogs can have a remarkable effect of their owners. They can teach people about compassion and unconditional love. I once had a worried mother write to me about her teenage daughter who was fast going off the rails. My aura reading of the girl suggested that allowing her to re-home an unwanted dog would have a good effect on her. But both her mum and I were amazed that within a few weeks of finding her dog friend, the daughter reverted to her old happy, generous self and turned her back on the gangs she had been starting to hang around with.

A dog can also help those who are painfully shy or socially inept to find the confidence to mix and talk more. Most people you meet will be drawn to your dog first, and so a painfully shy person can hide behind that in the beginning.

Evidence also shows that dogs have an amazing effect on children who are on the autistic spectrum, giving them a friend they can trust and confide in without fear of them saying something upsetting back. There are thousands of dogs needing a home and you only have to visit a re-homing kennel to become bewitched by them and find your child a suitable companion.

The Right Owner Can Change a Dog

You can buy interactive toys for your dog to stimulate his basic skills. These mostly consist of some sort of puzzle that your dog needs to solve to get a food reward.

If your dog has the right natural aptitude he can exercise his working skills, and the breeds that demonstrate these can sometimes be unexpected. For instance, most people don't realize that Rottweilers are great natural herders if given the chance to implement their skills. Look deeper into the breed characteristics of your dog and focus on the little-known talents he may have to offer in a working environment.

Agility training is a great way to exercise both your dog's body and his brain, and also strengthen the bond between you. Training your dog to negotiate an obstacle course with you running alongside giving encouragement is great fun, too.

Your pet can also become a 'therapy dog'. Dogs with the right temperament can provide invaluable comfort to people who are ill or confined in homes, hospitals and hospices. The joy on a patient's face when they get to cuddle or pet a dog for the first time in years, perhaps since they were children, is immeasurable. This way your dog can become a real hero and satisfy his soul's need to help to enrich the lives of others.

Immortality

Dogs will often lead us to them when they're reborn and want us to find them again. So, if you're hoping for this, watch for signs. These can take the form of strange 'coincidences' relating to your old dog's name, or date of birth or passing. You might keep seeing the same number everywhere you look or be woken at a certain time night after night. You might keep seeing the same combination of colours, telling you what colour coat to expect. In my case, one thing was an advert for puppies that I kept thinking I'd thrown away, only to find it back on the table.

All these things can add up and lead you to the right puppy. But if you think you've found him, how will you know for sure? Not everyone's lucky enough to get the physical evidence that I did, but I believe the eyes really are the windows to the soul. So if you think you're re-encountering the same dog soul you've known before, there will be recognition there. Take time to make eye contact and try a little telepathy by mentally asking the puppy to do something specific.

Communicating with Your Dog

Why not make a new start in communicating with your own beloved dog? A lot of people make the mistake of treating their dog as a baby. This isn't a problem as long as you acknowledge that there is more to your dog than this. You have to first honour the animal, then the dog, then the breed and finally your individual pet. If you can do this, one-to-one close communication is the next step. Recognize that your dog isn't just a small furry person, he's much more than that. As an animal he has all his intuition and instincts intact, unlike humans. He has senses of smell and hearing that are far more sensitive than yours, and as such he's much more aware of the natural world than you are. This means that most of the time your dog exists in a different world from you, so you have to respect his extra abilities and tune back into as many of your own instincts and intuitions that you can, if you really want to communicate with him. We still have these abilities. They're just buried beneath our civilized veneer.

You know your dog already, and all you need to do now in order to communicate is to get to know him even better. Take time out to observe his behaviour, his reaction to other dogs and people. Learn to be a body-language detective and mirror the little movements and expressions that your dog uses. Watch how he places his body instead of using words when he wants something and learn this hidden language. Take some time to sit quietly with your dog, just connecting in a mental way, not physically and not emotionally. Send your dog a message, such as to go somewhere or to come closer to you. For instance, if they're a retriever, send them an image of a certain toy and see if you can get them to fetch it. Or ask your dog to 'telegraph' to you an image of what they want, whether it's 'walkies' or some food or to play. Their reaction to whatever you choose to respond with will soon tell you if you 'heard' them correctly. If you can progress and establish a strong mental rapport like this, it can come in very useful should your dog ever go missing. I've had reports from people who've been able to find their dogs this way. The dog is able to send a mental image to its owner of the place and people where it is located, so that you are able to successfully track him down. It's even possible that a dog used to connecting with a human this way could give his rescuer important information about his owner or where he should be taken.

There's no doubt that humans and dogs have a special bond that goes back thousands of years. We all know that dogs have changed dramatically, due to their domestication by humans, but it is also a fact that dogs have shaped our journey towards civilization, too. When dogs became part of our ancestors' lives, they no longer needed to stay constantly on the alert for predators and enemies because the dogs took over that role, leaving the humans with more time to develop in other ways. The dogs also made hunting parties much more efficient with their presence, so people ate better, which may have enabled their brains to evolve more quickly.

Professor Colin Groves of the Australian National University in Canberra, said: '*The human–dog relationship amounts to a very long-lasting symbiosis. Dogs acted as humans' alarm systems, trackers and hunting aides, garbage disposal facilities, hot water bottles, and children's guardians and playmates. Humans provided dogs with food and security. The relationship was stable over 100,000 years or so, and intensified in the Holocene into mutual domestication. Humans domesticated dogs and dogs domesticated humans.*'

So, not only have dogs helped humankind throughout the centuries by being their right hand in battle, sacrificing themselves in fires and fights with predators in order to save their masters, and dedicating their lives to aiding the blind and the deaf and disabled, but they've also been responsible for changing the way we live and have even caused changes in our brains. For instance, some scientists, such as Lindsay Ellsworth, believe that interaction with dogs can release dopamine and other 'feel good' chemicals into human brains, which in some cases can even reverse negative changes caused by drug use. Our success as a species is directly related to the presence of domesticated dogs. They truly are the epitome of the phrase, 'forever faithful'.

CHAPTER 2

All about Cats

Some people find it hard to believe that cats are intelligent beings, here to share our wonderful planet with us, and instead think they of them as mere beasts, here for us to treat – and unfortunately, in some cases, mistreat – as we will. Sadly, many people still think this way, but of course it's not true. According to medical research, the brain structure of humans and cats is very similar, which doesn't of course means that cats would make intelligent people, or vice versa. The most intelligent cat breed, when tested, is the sphynx, which received a 10 out of 10 rating. These cats are closely followed by the Balinese, Bengal, colourpoint shorthair, Havana brown, Javanese, Oriental and Siamese.

Why not devote some time to increasing your cat's intelligence, and also his enjoyment of life. Conventional training, for example to teach your dog to 'sit', would be to press them down into the sit position while giving the command. This doesn't work well with cats. Instead, hold a treat in your closed hand just above the cat's head height. If they stand on their hind feet to reach, don't give them the treat. Wait until they either sit because they're puzzled, or to raise their heads slightly, and then say 'sit' and give them the treat. After a while they will associate the word with the deed and the reward.

Test it Out

There are many interactive cat toys that purport to test their intelligence, but you can devise simple tests of your own.

1. Show your cat a card with a picture of a dog on it. Dogs are not able to perceive or understand 2D images like this, but some cats can. If your cat reacts to the picture in some way, either by showing fear or attraction (if it likes dogs), then it has shown understanding.

2. Hold up two pictures of birds – one in your left hand, and one in your right, both facing the cat. If the cat goes to the one on its right, then it shows itself to be a left-brained, logical thinker. If it prefers the one on its left then it is a right-brained creative type.

3. Use the cup game. Place a titbit on the floor and cover it with an egg cup or something similar. Then put two empty egg cups down and mix them all up. See if your cat can pick the one concealing the titbit.

4. Put your cat's favourite treats in a box that requires a simple latch to be operated, or a button to be pressed to open it. Make sure you have your cat's attention and open the box, clearly showing how it's done. Give your cat a treat. Repeat this several times, then open it again, but don't give your cat a treat. Close the box and walk away. An intelligent cat will try to mimic what you did, and the cleverest will actually open it.

Your Psychic Cat

Cats have been regarded as mystical by many races since the time of the ancients. With their elliptical eyes and mysterious ways, it's not surprising. These beliefs have caused cats to be adored and reviled, revered and persecuted, but today we can appreciate the magic they bring to our lives without fear, and if we open our hearts and minds we just might find that cats are every bit as enigmatic as we like to think they are.

Spirit-seeing Cats and Orbs

Cats are very spiritual and have all their intuitive capabilities intact, unlike us, so they often see things we don't. If your cat often sits looking at a fixed point, and then seems to follow an unseen 'something' around the room, then consider that you may have an orb or even a ghostly visitor you're not aware of. If your cat uncharacteristically wakes you up in the middle of the night, it may be that he can sense the presence of a passed-over loved one.

I've known cats that have acted very strangely when a companion has died, too. One such cat had a dog for a friend, the cat being the older of the two. When the dog died the cat mourned so much the owners thought they might have to have her put to sleep. But one night the cat followed an unseen something up the stairs and they found her passed away peacefully on the bed. They were convinced the dog's spirit had come back for his friend.

Capture It on Film

Don't let this sort of behaviour scare you. There are many wonders in the universe that we don't understand. Knowledge and understanding are power, so take steps to find out what your cat is seeing and sensing. Use a digital camera to take photos whenever your cat behaves in these strange ways and you might be able to capture an orb, or maybe several, on the photograph. If there's nothing odd on the photo, it may just be that your cat's been getting bored and is doing his tricks just to pass the time or even to get your attention. But if you do get orbs in snaps taken at this time, you can be sure that 'someone' is using your cat to try and tell you something. Interesting orbs are those that appear to move or seem to be behind an object, because they can't be dismissed as marks on the lens.

Do Cats Have Angels?

If you believe in angels, and that you have a guardian angel, then perhaps cats have angels, too. Some of the stories I've been sent, and included in this book, suggest that cats can become divine beings. This might be for a short time, for instance in a time of need, or a cat might have an angelic presence for its whole life.

How did you find your cat?

Everything I said previously about dogs and angels, and the fact that there's a reason you and your pet found each other, applies equally to cats. Think about how your life has changed since he or she arrived. Perhaps you were able to begin a wonderful new relationship after previous heartbreak, or your finances took a turn for the better. Could your cat have played a part in these events? Perhaps you were led to your particular cat because their name resonated with you? Or perhaps, having lost out on the kitten you'd set your heart on, you suddenly received a message from a friend about a litter of kittens which hadn't been homed and were about to be taken to the local shelter? Did your cat just arrive in your life unexpectedly – as a stray, or perhaps injured or abandoned, and you decided to help him?

Everything happens for a reason, and you and your cat coming together is no exception. Think about all the things that have changed about your life, and his, by each other's presence. Who knows – you may find that you and your cat both have angels by your side!

Mystical Cats

Cats have always been considered strange and magical, and beliefs vary depending on geography. For instance, in America it's considered unlucky if a black cat crosses your path, whereas in the UK and Japan, the reverse is true. Here are some legends from around the world.

Latvia: Black cats are considered to be a manifestation of the god Rungis, who can bring a good harvest, so seeing a black cat in your grain silos is considered good luck.

Japan: A cat with a black spot is believed to be carrying the soul of a passed-over loved one and will bring good luck.

Burma: They believe that someone's soul will go into a cat and be transported safely by the cat to paradise.

Scandinavia: The goddess Freya had a chariot pulled by cats, so leaving offerings to them would ensure a good harvest.

Greece: It was believed that the goddess Hecate used the symbol of a black cat to materialize. People still leave offerings for cats at crossroads to ask the goddess for good luck.

Ireland: It was believed that certain cats, called King Cats, guard some sort of treasure. They were thought to be fairy beings who appreciate gifts, in exchange for which they might lead you to their treasure.

France: Their mystical cat was called a magician cat and if treated with great respect it would bring its master good fortune.

Technicolour Dream Cats

Dreaming of cats of certain colours have particular meanings:

- A calico cat indicates that you will soon make a new friend.

- A tortoiseshell cat means you have new love coming.

- A tabby indicates a good time to move, as you'll be lucky with property.

- A black and white cat means your children are entering a lucky phase.

Has Your Cat Been Here Before?

Did you ever look at your cat and think, 'You're way too clever for a cat?' Or perhaps you never intended to have a cat at all, but were drawn and seemingly directed to one that you found impossible to resist, almost like you already knew it? Do you have a special affinity with cats, with them seeming to treat you as one of their own, or do people often call you cat-like, saying you move like a cat, or have feline grace and characteristics? Anyone who looks into the eyes of a cat and says, 'It's just a cat,' should open their minds and look a little deeper, for a cat is often much more than it appears.

Is Your Cat Immortal?

My research for my books has shown me that animals have souls, just like us, and are therefore immortal. They can also return to their owners in a new body – be reincarnated. Cats that return time after time to be with the same owner are closely connected to them on a spiritual level. Not only that but cat souls can also eventually choose the ultimate challenge and become human. I say ultimate challenge, because being human and remaining spiritually attuned is much harder as a human than it is as a cat, because cats are born with all instincts and intuitions intact. We on the other hand, have to relearn them.

How Can You Tell?

If you think your cat might have returned to you in a new body, there's a way to test it out. Your soul-level connection will give you the ability to communicate without words. To try this at home, you need to sit quietly, close your eyes, slow your breathing and try to surround yourself with peaceful energy. Think of a beautiful place that you love and picture it in detail in your mind's eye. This will help you to tune into your subconscious. Once you feel totally relaxed, try 'thinking' to your cat. If the cat is outside, try calling him to you with your mind alone. If the cat's with you, try 'thinking' him to bring you a toy, climb on your lap, go to another room or just go to sleep. When you feel you've connected, open your eyes and see what's happened. If your cat has done as you 'thought', then it's almost certain that you have lived together before.

Your Cat's Intuition

Cats That Sense Illness

Recently the BBC published a report about a cat called Oscar, who had apparently predicted the deaths of some care-home residents by curling up beside them. Some people feel there may be a supernatural explanation for this, while others say it's more to do with the cat's amazing sense of smell.

Much research has been done regarding dogs and disease detection, but there are more and more documented cases of cats having the same ability. A woman from Texas told me that her cat had persistently pawed and then started to scratch her side. Eventually she was so concerned that she went to her doctor, only to discover that she had ovarian cancer and was able to be treated before the disease caught hold. Other people have told me how their cat predicted the imminent death of a pet chicken or the family dog by cuddling up to it for a few hours before it died.

Don't Get Carried Away

This isn't something I'd recommend owners to try to replicate with their cats, just because it's very easy to become paranoid and think that every time their cat sniffs them, he's detecting cancer or diabetes or something equally scary. If your cat repeatedly paws or sniffs a part of you for no apparent reason, it's a good idea to be vigilant, but don't take it to extremes. This is because it doesn't seem easy to train cats to do this on command, as cats are inherently less easy to train than dogs, and so you could get a lot of potentially worrying false results by trying to use your cat to give you a 'health check'.

Your Cat's Personal Development

Every single creature on the Earth, including us, has come here to learn and progress. We all need to feel, even if subconsciously, that we're developing, otherwise there's little point in us being here. The same can be said of your cat. Every cat, from those with apparently little intelligence, to those that seem almost human in their understanding and reasoning powers, need to learn, so that they can eventually return to spirit, changed for the better. Cats are very adept learners because of their prevalent high intelligence, and by teaching them, you'll also be nurturing their need to improve.

Therapy Cats

Most people think of dogs when they think of a therapy pet, but cats are being used more and more. There are reasons for this. Cats are quieter generally than dogs and so they are less disruptive for seriously ill people. Also, they have an inbuilt, relaxing, vibration system – their purr! This means that they generate big responses from people who have hearing disabilities and those with impaired senses. Cats chosen for therapy must meet certain criteria. They must be relaxed and docile, and tolerant of new places and contacts.

If your cat has the right temperament it can be trained to do this work. Obviously, claws can be a lethal weapon, and you might worry that your cat would have to be declawed to be used with vulnerable people, but that would be cruel, and indeed is illegal in the UK. Instead there are some excellent bootees that your cat can comfortably wear to safeguard patients.

Therapy cats need to be trained and qualified and can then be used in hospitals, respite homes, care homes and nursing homes. Your reward is to see the patients' and residents' eyes light up when your cat walks in. Some of the people may have had to lose their beloved cat when they became ill, or had to become a resident in a home, so you have a chance to bring a lot of joy back into their lives.

The Wild Animal in Your Cat

Sometimes the only drawback to having a cat is that they kill pretty creatures such as birds. Many people like to feed their birds, especially at very cold times of the year, and it's distressing when you discover that your bird feeders are some sort of acrobatic fast food restaurant for your cat, who'll like nothing more that leaping 2 metres (6 feet) into the air to grab a fleeing sparrow.

We've gone to great lengths in our house to do two things. We have a cat that doesn't chase birds (some breeds naturally don't) and we've erected an aviary to cover our feeders, to prevent neighbourhood cats killing them. Can you do these things, too? Our aviary is just a cheap 2 x 1 metre (6 x 3 feet) wire cage, with holes cut in to allow small birds (up to woodpecker size) through. They learned to use it very quickly. Once inside, neither cat, nor sparrow hawk for that matter, can get them, unless they panic and fly out while the hunter's still lurking.

The Hunter

If you don't have a cat yet, check with rescue centres to see if they have any orphaned kittens. Of course, it is a terrible shame when kittens lose their mothers, but you can turn this tragedy into a positive. Many cat owners aren't aware that if they aren't trained to hunt by their mothers, and if their owners don't encourage them to play with feathered toys, cats will often never grow up to hunt birds. So, bring up your kitten differently. Focus his hunting by playing with toys that only represent anything you're happy for him to hunt.

If you already have an adult cat that hunts and you'd rather he didn't, there isn't much you can do to change his nature, except by playing with him enough to keep him tired, both mentally and physically. When dealing with entire (non-neutered) cats, whether they are queens or toms, it's a good idea to remember that they are essentially wild animals. To have a wild animal living in your house will always require some compromise, and you'll need to take steps to respect their feral nature.

Treat your cat with dignity and yet always be their leader. If your cat is restless and aggressive, use his intelligence to teach him things. Brain exercise will calm your cat down and make sure he stays close to home and doesn't let his curiosity cause him problems.

Communication

Why not make a new start in communicating with your beloved cat? Humans tend to communicate through sheer vocalization and have often lost their ability to read body language. Cats, on the other hand, have very well-developed communication skills and use a complex system of facial expression, touch, scent and body language. Make sure you pay attention to all aspects of your cat when trying to communicate.

The Voice

Cats use a very large vocabulary and it's up to us to learn it. They have a wide range through mew to yowl and by careful observation of what your cat is doing when it makes a sound, and how it reacts after the sound, you can start to build knowledge of what each noise means. After a while you'll know immediately wherever your cat wants to be let out or fed, cuddled or left alone. All animals appreciate an effort made to communicate with them so that they are understood and will become closer to their owners as a result, and cats are no different.

Think It

Take time to sit quietly near your cat, and just try to connect mentally (rather than physically or emotionally) with them. As mentioned earlier in this chapter (*see page 53*), try to 'think' a message to them, such as asking them to fetch something or come to you. Also ask them to 'telegraph' you an image of something they want, such as food or a favourite toy. Their reaction to whatever you choose to respond with will soon tell you if you 'heard' them correctly.

Establishing this kind of mental rapport can be invaluable should your cat ever go missing. I've heard from people who've been able to locate their lost cat in this way. The cat is able to send to its owner a mental image of the place it's in and people it's with, and as cats often get themselves trapped inside empty buildings, such as garages and sheds, this can be life-saving. It works both ways too – it's possible that a cat used to connecting with a human in this way could give his rescuer important information about his owner, and where he should be taken.

CHAPTER 3

Hero Cats and Dogs

Dogs have been our companions and protectors throughout history. Since the first wolves and jackals overcame their fear and crept into the firelight of humans' camps to share our food, they've been guardians, hunters, trackers, herders and, most of all, friends with people. They are renowned as being natural rescuers and protectors and are featured in many films and books doing just that. Some people who don't believe dogs have souls might explain this by saying that their owners and family (and other pets) are part of their pack, and therefore should be protected from harm and danger. But this doesn't always make sense. There is no doubt from the following stories that dogs feel love for their families and sometimes will also act compassionately to people and animals they don't even know.

Perhaps cats are less likely heroes on the face of it, because they appear to be much more self-reliant than dogs, less needy and more able to exist alone without a pack. I don't think there's ever been a movie about a cat performing the deeds of a 'Lassie' and saving 'Timmy' when he had fallen down the well. Conversely, cats are often the chosen pet of the villains of the piece: Cruella de Vil had a cat, and Blofeld (the Bond baddie) had a cat. I can only find two movies with anything approaching a hero cat in them, and those are *The Incredible Journey* (in which the cat had to co-star with two dogs) and *Shrek*, in which the sword-wielding hero cat had to compete with a mouthy donkey and a dragon for the status of hero.

It's not the fault of cats that they haven't been seen as the 'good guys' as throughout history cats have been portrayed as the companion and familiar of witches, with a black cat crossing your path thought to be unlucky in some cultures. Some poor defenceless cats were actually burned with 'witches', for fear that if left alive they would become possessed by their dead owners. This nastiness happened mostly in medieval times, when night-time was considered to be a dangerous period – of course, cats were known to have apparent supernatural powers such as seeing in the dark and were abroad in the dark, so they became associated with danger.

However, not every culture has vilified cats. In ancient Egypt the goddess Bast was always depicted as a cat and for some time in Egypt one could be sentenced to death for harming a cat. Of course, this probably only served to enhance their reputation for being dangerous!

Cats tend to spend a lot of time alone and when in a household they accept their family, rather than adoring them. However, the stories that follow in this book prove that there are some people–cat relationships that go far above the norm, and that cats enjoying such special bonds with their owners will certainly go above and beyond self-survival with those they love, and in so doing they have certainly proved that they have souls.

Wise and mystical, courageous and strong-willed, cats are a force to be reckoned with and this power can be turned into hero capabilities. So I was only a little surprised that when I requested stories about cats who had performed heroically, I was swamped with just as many of heroic tales for them as I was for dogs.

Jenny's story

One day I was travelling from a small town on my way back to Chicago, with my white kitten Wrigley. It was a snowy, windy, cold winter morning with severe blizzard conditions and suddenly I lost control of my jeep. It's amazing how, in a split second, your life can change. Before I knew it, my jeep was spinning around like a top and then it teetered and began to roll over and over violently, several times. Only one thought raced through my mind and that was: *I'm going to die.*

Somehow, I survived and got out, but to my horror Wrigley was missing. After suffering through a night of physical pain and horrifying nightmares, the next morning I decided to return to the accident site with my parents, in the hope of finding Wrigley. Whether he was dead or alive, I needed closure to this nightmare. After a gruelling search in the wind, snow and flesh-eating cold, I'm overjoyed to say that I found the little guy, having almost mistaken him for a cluster of odd-shaped stones in the distance. He was half-frozen and his face was bloody. I fell to the ground clutching him in my arms and, can you believe it, he started purring! We took Wrigley to the nearest vet. He'd broken his front left leg and had to have a metal rod put in to set the bone straight. He also had to have part of his tail amputated and a snippet of his left ear clipped due to frostbite – but he'd survived. We both had. Every day I look at him and thank God that we survived and, as cheesy as it sounds, I truly believe we have a special bond.

You can imagine the scene, with Jenny looking for her cat in the white-out. You would have thought it would be impossible to ever see him as he was as white as the snow. But she did. Some instinct, or was it him mentally crying out to her made her investigate the rocks?

Carole's story

Last year in February I thought maybe I could give a good home to a blind or deaf dog from Spain. I live in Germany, but I knew there were so many poor dogs in other countries, desperately looking for homes, just as I was desperately looking for a dog I could really make a difference to, but it had to be 'my dog' if you know what I mean.

Somehow, I landed on a website belonging to a lovely woman called Maria, managed by a woman here in Germany. She had a few dogs not in Spain but in Greece that really needed a home. I looked through them all, each one more pitiful than the next. There seems to be such terrible cruelty in the world towards street dogs. Then I suddenly found myself looking at a middle-sized street mutt called Salina. She had a smashed front leg. The woman from the dog sanctuary had been at the vet's with her dog when Salina was brought in by a passerby. They asked for her to be put down, as they felt sorry for her, dragging her leg around and in pain. Apparently, she had crawled over to Maria and licked her hand, as if to say, 'Help me.' The next photo was of her after she'd had her leg amputated, and I was amazed to see an orb over her shoulder. I immediately knew this was my dog, and the look in her eyes was one I recognized.

I wrote to them immediately about Salina, and they soon phoned me up to arrange a home visit, to see if we were suitable. Also, I had to raise some money to bring her over. I sold my flute (I am a music teacher) and they were kind enough to give me a bit of a discount on the transport costs. The woman who rescued Salina flew her over four weeks later with four other dogs and we met them at Düsseldorf airport. The dogs were, of course, totally scared and confused. We managed to get Salina into the car, and from that second she was mine. She cuddled up to me, put her head on my lap and went straight to sleep.

When we got her home she was immediately clean, as if already house-trained, and she's never had an accident in the house. She decided she should sleep on the sofa, and sometimes on my bed, and she totally rules the roost! She has an incredible character and likes to chew shoes and carpets, and is very playful, but for a street dog she's adapted really well. Everyone loves her and comments on the look in her eyes. She is now two, and we have had her for nearly a year. I honestly think we were always meant to find each other. Incredibly, I found a new flute really cheaply for half the price just afterwards, so I never even missed the other one!

Some partnerships with dogs and cats are just meant to be, and as the song says, 'there ain't no mountain high enough' to keep them apart. The same thing happens with human soulmates, and pet soulmates are no different.

Ted's story

I was at the vet because my old cat had died. I had no plans on getting a new cat, but then I saw one called Stella, literally sliding across the vinyl floor. She had no back feet and no pads, and she was just gliding all over the floor. I thought I should have her because of all my work with the disabled and sick. It turned out that she'd had OCD. She'd scratch her head, all the time, ripping the skin off. Apparently, her old owners thought that if they declawed her back feet, she would stop. That didn't really work as her feet got infected and they had to be amputated. At that point the old owners were angry at the vet for the bills and dumped the cat. That story alone was enough to make me want to take her, so I did. I brought Stella home, and my girlfriend at the time, who was a vet, said we should put her on anti-anxiety meds. That seemed to make her life somewhat more normal. She's still a bit of a wacky cat, but the meds stopped her repetitive behaviour.

I'm the artist-in-residence at UCLA Medical School. I often speak to doctor-and-patient groups. In my presentations I show slides of people who have major scars, and subsequent disabilities, and I tell their stories. The last slide is always of Stella, showing her amputated paws. After the audience has watched 20–25 slides of people with horrid deformities in perfect silence, up pops the Stella slide, and everyone gasps, 'Awwwww'. This always gives me the opportunity to start a discussion on how we as humans react to the pain and suffering of other people versus how we react to animals in the same boat. Why would we be more likely to feel sorry for a sick cat than for a sick person? I don't know, but Stella has become a very important part of my talks.

This little cat is a 'teacher soulmate' of Ted's, who came into his life to show him how to teach others to cope with disabilities, both their own and other peoples'.

Consuelo's story

I stopped my truck to check out a small, funny-looking terrier sitting in the middle of the road. She looked up at me with a huge smile on her face and then disappeared from view. Thinking she might be under my truck, I got out to double-check and walked all the way around it to make sure she wasn't there. When I got back to the open driver's door, she was sitting behind the steering wheel, grinning.

I only ever crated Abby once, during a visit to my son, Bobby. He had a dog, so to avoid any problems I crated Abby while we went shopping. When we came back she was on the bed in the guest room. She'd pulled my brand new shirt through the front and used it to pop the crate door open.

I'm an artist and a TV craft show asked me to film two segments for it. While we were setting up my studio for the shoot, my husband, Joe, was putting Abby through her paces for the director. The director was so impressed that she filmed it, and when the show aired, there was Abby in the middle of the segment. She got her own fan-mail after that.

As the years went by, Abby started to show clear signs of ageing. She developed liver disease, which our vet treated but couldn't cure. The worst thing was that my brilliant, genius dog developed severe senility, which we couldn't treat. The dog who had mastered more tricks than several other dogs combined now rarely responded to her own name. One day she wandered away, and for five days we walked up and down the roads and through the woods bordering our home, searching desperately. On the fifth day we got a phone call from a woman who'd had found a dog on the street adjoining ours. It was Abby. They'd found her walking in circles in the middle of the road. We were extremely lucky that these kind people had picked her up. We were thrilled to be reunited with her, but soon after she let me know it was time to make plans to say goodbye. The day of the appointment Joe went out and brought home her favourite food in the world – an ice-cream cone. She hadn't had this treat in a long time because of her special diet, so when she realized what it was, she gave us her old, goofy smile and ate most of it.

The vet asked us how old Abby was. We could only guess at her age, but the vet told us she thought Abby was at least 18! Within a minute our girl was gone. We hugged and kissed her for the last time, then left. This was one of the hardest things I've ever done, but I know it was the right thing. I believe ensuring your pet has a kind, humane death is part of the responsibility you take on when you bring them home. After all her years of loving us unconditionally, she deserved to die painlessly and with dignity. Abby was cremated, so when it's my turn to go, her ashes will be mixed with mine and spread over the Catskill Mountains. I'll never forget that amazing dog and all the time we spent together.

Consuelo is so right. While making the choice to end our pet's life will be one of the hardest we ever have to make – and one that will haunt us – we must remember that an animal that can no longer 'be' that animal, but has become just a mere shadow of itself, can't be happy and fulfilled. It can't read a book or while away the day watching TV. Our pets are in our hands, and they rely on us to know when they've had enough, and not cling onto them for selfish reasons. But it is so hard – the greatest gift of love.

Barbara's story

I should have realized that my cat Keyo was different from the start. Upon her arrival, my husband had looked at this little kitten and asked, 'Can she catch mice?' Keyo had looked right back at him, then raced into the crawl space and returned with a mouse about 30 seconds later. She didn't kill the mouse, but dropped it live at my husband's feet. His face was a picture. Had this kitten understood every word that he said or what? She took one look at the litter box we had set up for her, walked to the door and meowed to go out. She returned a few moments later after using the huge outdoor litter box. For the 23 years she was with us, she'd meow to go out when needed to, never used the indoor litter and never had an accident.

The two huge golden retrievers from next door ran after her into our yard one day. I was terrified and scooped her up immediately and ran for the house. I put her down but before I could close the door on her she ran back outside hissing and spitting. In the end the two dogs went home, tails between their legs, whimpering.

Keyo disappeared for a week within a month of our bringing her home. With a broken heart I put away her dish and resigned myself to having lost a very special kitten. A full week later, during a raging thunderstorm in the middle of the night, we heard a whimper at the garage door. It was Keyo. She was skin and bones, with huge patches of missing fur, and so dehydrated she couldn't eat on her own, so we nursed her back to health. Within a week she was able to go outside once again. She went on a hunting frenzy once and I returned home to find an array of six or seven rodents lined up neatly at the garage door. I could almost hear her saying, 'I'll never be hungry again!'

Over her 23-year life she disappeared twice more (once for each home she shared with us). She always found her way back. Keyo had no patience for, 'Here kitty, kitty,' but she always came to a whistle. I've owned a lot of cats, but I've never had another like Keyo.

Cats are known to be independent and it takes a dedicated owner to envelop such a free spirit with love, but Barbara allowed her cat to be who she truly was, which is wonderful.

Penny's story

My husband, Mike, and I have a backyard that's well fenced in. It has had to be that way, as at the time our daughter Abigail was only four years old, and she was a naturally curious child and into everything. One day Mike was happily working in the vegetable plot and Abigail was playing in her sandpit. Mike suddenly heard our dog, Eclipse, barking as if all the bad guys in the world were trying to get in. He called out to her, but she wouldn't quit. Then she appeared at Mike's side and grabbed his trouser leg. She'd never ever laid a tooth on us before. She tried to drag Mike around behind the trees towards the road that ran outside our yard, and it was then he realized that Abigail had vanished from her play area. He ran around back and found she'd managed to open the gate and was about to set off on a dangerous adventure down the street. From that day, Eclipse was Abigail's guardian angel. As Abigail grew up they went everywhere together.

Some years later Eclipse was turning into an old dog and she didn't see or hear too well. We always made sure the gates were shut, just as we had when our daughter was small, only this time it was because of Eclipse and our concern for her.

One day we were all three of us sitting at the kitchen table having some coffee, when Abigail suddenly dropped her mug with a plonk onto the table, spilling the coffee. Without a word she jumped up, ran out the back door and down the back of the yard. We ran after her, puzzled. She'd gone straight out the back gate, and that's where we found her, by the side of the road, her arms round Eclipse. She'd got there just in time to grab our old dog before she walked unknowingly right in front of a car. It was like history repeating itself, and that's what I call a partnership! Eclipse won't be with us for much longer, I suppose, but when she goes her soulmate Abigail will be with her in spirit, by her side, of that there's no doubt. It will be the end of an era, but we'll never, ever forget Eclipse.

That brought tears to my eyes. Animals and children often have the most special relationships, and their communications can be extra strong.

Tina's story

My cat Rusty is a street rescue who was cuddly and lovable from the very first meow. The first day that he showed up I put food out for him because I thought he was a lost stray. The second day he showed up, I put food out again. This continued for about a week. On day eight (or thereabouts), Rusty started crossing the street. He stopped and turned around as though he were looking for something or someone. Within a minute or so I spotted another cat, who came to be called Crystal, pop out from the bushes. Rusty proceeded to cross the street periodically, checking to make sure Crystal was in tow. This went on for two more days before I realized that he was bringing her to my home for a reason. At the time I just figured it was his friend. As a cat person, I thought, what's one more?

Whenever I went to pick up Rusty, he lovingly came into my arms without hesitation. Crystal, on the other hand, would flee. It was at this point that I realized she was feral. Over the course of three days, Rusty was free to come and go in my home, and each day, Crystal came closer to the front door. It was as though Rusty was saying, 'Crystal, it's OK… this lady will help you.' (Sounds crazy, but in my heart, I could feel what was happening.)

After five days Crystal cautiously came into the house. She ate, slept, ate and slept. The morning that we were to go to the vet, Crystal became ill, vomiting blood. It was then that I realized she was sick. When she tested positive for diabetes and feline leukaemia, it was obvious that it was in Crystal's best interest for her to be put down. Rusty was a true hero for helping a feral friend find peace.

Prior to this, I'd not done any volunteer work because I was fighting my own battles with depression. Rusty helped me divert my attention from myself, in his attempts to help Crystal. I know he brought Crystal to me for help and, in the process, he helped me. Rusty has been a blessing to so many people. He's quiet, but very present and powerful. He has become a proud Pet Therapy Volunteer through the SPCA. We've visited hundreds of 'Give Kids the World' events, elderly patients at assisted living facilities and, most recently, went on a fundraiser outing. While Rusty has slowed down a bit these days, he still enjoys meeting the public and is fearless in crowds of people and dogs.

What a wonderful and compassionate soul Rusty showed himself to be! You can't read that story without admitting that cats and dogs do have souls, too.

Samantha's story

I'm paralysed in all four limbs, and I really thought my life was over until I was introduced to Cesar, my assistance dog. The way it worked is that Cesar chose me, by sitting next to me rather than next to any of the other potential recipients. For the first time in years, by walking my golden dog I've actually got a suntan and look healthier than I have for some time. Cesar trots happily alongside my motorized chair, and the two of us have made many new friends because no one can resist this beautiful dog.

One day we got a little too adventurous, and my chair just stopped in the middle of nowhere, down an unmade road that was just about smooth enough for my chair. I tried my mobile phone but it was out of signal. I didn't know what to do, but then I just kept telling Cesar, 'Go home!' He'd been trained, of course, not to pull hard on the chair, but after a while the desperation in my voice must have got through to him and he turned to face the chair and started walking backwards, digging his feet in to get traction. He hauled me several hundred yards up the road, being careful not to jerk too hard and tip me out. Finally, I was able to get a signal and ring for help. My mum and dad arrived to help me out. If it hadn't been for Cesar I would have been really stuck that day. As it was, it gave us all greater faith in him.

How on earth did this dog understand what he had to do? Was this one of those dogs that becomes divine for a few minutes in time?

Janine's story

My cat Hero was truly a hero to me. I suffer from ME, and as a result I miss out on a lot of things. People often pooh-poohed my illness, believing it to be purely psychosomatic. Not Hero, though. He knew that I really, genuinely needed help, and he gave it willingly, doing everything he could think of to make things better.

He did the most extraordinary things for me. He brought me presents – and not just dead prey like most cats, but sparkly things like tinsel or coloured paper, even though cats are not supposed to see colours well. He once brought me a tiny, round mirror; I couldn't imagine where he'd got that from. He could also open most doors, and somehow found a way to get right up to our balcony window so he could get inside the house. He had to use drainpipes and windowsills to do that. But his best trick was that he learned to answer the phone: when it rang he would knock it off its stand and go and get someone to answer it properly, even if we were in out the garden. He was truly amazing.

Hero showed great understanding of Janine's illness, more so than most people.

Heidi's story

I have a little Bichon Frise called Bubbles. I call her my little shadow because she's my constant companion, and we talk to each other. I run a spiritual and psychic development circle and work as a psychic artist and medium, and Bubbles likes to help whenever she can. A circle member and friend of mine had a bad hand with a raised, red lump on it that wouldn't go away. Bubbles always made a bee-line for him on his regular visits. She would insist on licking his bad hand over and over. This went on for some time, and we found it odd and so interesting. Eventually we decided it meant something, so he got his hand checked at the doctor's and it turned out that my good friend had skin cancer in the form of a growth on that hand! He's now had it treated, and goes for regular checks, but we're convinced Bubbles knew and was trying to heal him, as well as flagging up the danger of the problem. She still loves him and gives him cuddles, but no longer licks that hand, so we're sure he's clear of the cancer for good.

We know that animals, especially dogs and cats, can now be trained to scent out diseases in people. I think this proves that some of them have an innate talent for it that requires no training and these pets seem to be drawn to the owners who are going to need that talent.

Consuelo's story

My Persian cat, Maggie, came to live with us as a 12-week-old kitten. Always very affectionate and playful, the second anyone new would come to the house, she'd disappear.

My mother-in-law lived with us for five years due to poor health. As a kitten Maggie was very close to her, sleeping in her bed every night, but as she got older she decided that she'd rather sleep in my bed. She still spent a lot of time with Mom, but for some reason wouldn't go near her bed.

Eventually the time came when we knew the end was near, so a hospice nurse was brought in. Several minutes after the nurse arrived, Maggie came out from hiding and climbed into bed with Mom.

That whole night Maggie never left Mom's side. Then suddenly at 6 a.m. Maggie jumped up, licked Mom's face and left the room. Within five minutes Mom passed away. Many times since then we've found her sitting on the couch next to where we keep family pictures, staring at one of her and Mom together.

Maggie clearly had a very special connection with Consuelo's mother-in-law that even seems to have survived her passing.

Maria's story

My dog Topaz was a bit unusual. She was a Labrador that didn't like to swim; in fact, she was scared of water full stop. She didn't like to be bathed and would never go in a pond or a river. This was one reason why we got her – her first owner wanted a gundog, so a dog that wouldn't go near water wasn't any good to him. I didn't care, she was a wonderful dog and she and I used to roam around, growing up together.

When we were both 10 years old I had a bit of a mishap. I was round a neighbour's yard, having accidentally thrown Topaz's ball over the fence, and I'd gone to get it. They had a big pool, but it was covered up for the winter. They were away on vacation. The ball was right there on the cover and I couldn't quite reach it. I found the net they used to scoop leaves off the water and I leaned out, further and further, just half an inch from the ball. I'm sure you've guessed – just as I thought I'd got it, I overbalanced. I screamed as I fell onto the pool cover, but I wasn't too scared as I thought I could just roll back to the side and off. What I hadn't realized was that they hadn't fixed the sides of the cover, so as I landed on it the whole thing folded up and closed over my head, pushing me under the water. I was a strong swimmer, but I just couldn't get away from the embrace of the wet plastic that was dragging me under. I didn't know which way was up, and I really thought I was going to die.

Suddenly they was a mighty flopping noise right next to me, and another body started thrashing around, bumping me. It was Topaz! I couldn't believe that my dog had finally overcome her fear of water and jumped in to save me. Somehow, she managed to grab the cover and drag it off me. That left the two of us floundering in the water, and this time I was able to help *her*, because she really couldn't swim. Finally, both bedraggled, we made it to the side and pushed and pulled each other out somehow. That dog overcame a terror she had in order to save me, and that makes her a real hero, because she felt the fear and did it anyway!

I love Maria's story because it shows so well the wonderful need and 'rightness' of some partnerships between human and dog. My intuition tells me that Topaz may have actually been Maria's mother in a past life – whether they were both human or both animal, I don't know.

Melanie's story

I have diabetes, and when I was younger I wasn't too hot at checking my sugar levels. A couple of times I keeled over and would have been in big trouble if my cat Mikey hadn't stood over me and yowled the place down. I was a student at the time, and although Mikey was really the boarding school's cat, I called him mine because he almost always hung around me. The other students got used to coming running when they heard the yowling. I lost count over the years at school of how often Mikey must have saved my life, but I am sure I wouldn't be here today, aged over 60, if it hadn't been for him. I was really sorry to leave that school, as I never saw Mikey again after that. But maybe he was helping someone else after I left. He was probably saving someone else's life over and over. Those times were 50 years ago now, but I still remember my hero cat.

If we're lucky we get a memory like this – of that one animal that genuinely changed our life or, as in this case, saved it, then left it. I'm almost certain that this pet will have returned to Melanie at some point in her life, maybe in a new body after it had passed away and been reborn!

Stevie's story

I was the kid everyone picked on. I was fat, there was no question about that, and the more miserable I was, the more food I ate. I never went out except to go to school, and I think if things hadn't changed I would for sure have had a heart attack aged 18 or thereabouts. As it was, a furry friend saved me.

One Christmas Eve my mom brought a scruffy little bundle home with her. She'd seen him in a pet shop and felt sorry for him. It was love at first sight for me. I thought he was going to be a small dog, but the big paws should have given me a clue. With mom feeding him up, he grew to be a very big dog, even when he was still young. Mom was happy for me to take responsibility for him and I called him Chuck. I started walking, short distances at first, then miles. I had to, really, because if I didn't then Chuck would chew up my room and sometimes my clothes. After a while I wasn't thinking much about school, where it used to give me nightmares. All I could think about was going training.

Chuck started to win prizes for obedience and I started to lose weight. Eventually the kids at school met Chuck and me out walking, and their attitude to me changed completely after that. He was a big dog, but they liked him – although it's true to say they probably wouldn't have wanted to get on his bad side, I guess!

Chuck didn't drag me out of a fire or anything dramatic like that. He did turn my life around, though, and I'll never forget what he did for me.

Oh Stevie! Chuck may not have dragged you out of a fire but he made you who you are, and sometimes that's just as important.

Anna's story

I never really wanted a cat. I got mine, Queen, by accident. I used to live in a flat above a restaurant and there were a lot of mice, some of which made their way upstairs to my home. They were running under my bed at night and I couldn't take it anymore, so I got a cat.

When I got Queen home she was extremely scared and hid away in the corners. I'd never had a cat before and I didn't know what to do, so I just provided her with food and a litter tray, and waited. I used to talk to her like she was a newborn baby, giving her a lot of love and attention. After some time she started coming into my bed and sleeping with me, but anytime I had any visitors she was so scared she would hide again.

After a few months I moved to the beautiful countryside, and from that day she started going out and enjoying life. Our relationship started growing, too, and now she's become the most important thing in my life. Sometimes when she's out for a long time and I worry, I just sit down and start calling her in my thoughts, and after a few minutes she's back. Until recently she wasn't a cat I could cuddle, but one day I just asked her, 'Could you give me a kiss, please?' and I was so shocked when she immediately rubbed her head against mine. I was thinking, she can't understand what I'm saying to her. Oh how mistaken I was!

One night she saved my life. I was asleep and she woke me up at night screaming so loudly by the kitchen door that I woke up. I opened the kitchen door and found I had a gas leak!

After a trip away I got very depressed because I couldn't get over all the abuse I'd seen suffered by animals in other countries. I tried to save a few cats on my trip, but nobody really cared about them. So I decided to take in another little kitten, and I brought Jasmine home. Queen was so angry that she didn't come back for three days, but now, almost a year later, she's very protective of Jasmine, teaching her hunting and not allowing her out when it's raining.

Queen is the most special cat in the whole universe. I love little Jasmine also, but with Queen I've got this connection that I can't explain. She's everything to me.

This is how it happens, I am the same – I love all my pets, but some are just a spark of my soul and they are as close and as vital to me as my arm or my leg.

Sarah's story

'Tammy Tam Tams' is my dog's name. She barks, she's constantly into everything, she's forever getting under my feet; but despite this she really is one in a million, and I wouldn't have her any other way. Tammy is a girly-girl, known in the area for wiggling her hips and flapping her ears as she shows off her bright pink knitted sweater down the street! She is a strong character with a real drive for what she wants, and it's thanks to these qualities that she got her through the first three years of her innocent life, where she suffered mental and physical abuse at the hands of her previous owners. She was beaten, tortured, teased and tormented with food, which made into a nervous wreck and terrified of men. But this came to an end when she came to live with me. With a lot of work and time, she learned that it was safe to trust and respect me, which resulted in a close, life-long bond of mutual love and loyalty which we shared all her life. We had our hardships and triumphs to overcome, but together we came through. Shortly after Tammy arrived she intervened in a rape, scaring off the rapist. And another time she scared away burglars while we were in the house on our own.

Some years earlier I had suffered a paralysing spinal accident, leaving me wheelchair-bound. Tammy stood up to the mark and was my tower of strength with all the love she gave me. While Tams learned to adapt to a new way of life around me, she inspired me to keep going because I knew what she had previously endured. By working together we even learned how I could take her out for walks, even if that did mean often hitching a lift on my lap as she got older!

Sadly, because of the physical abuse she went through as a puppy, she suffered with numerous painful medical conditions. She had severe spondylitis, kidney and liver function problems, joint stiffness, seizures, vestibular syndrome and arthritis. She also had dementia, which unfortunately took her back to her young days, but the bond we shared got her through these episodes. She cried when I left her and went absolutely crazy when I arrived home. She had some pretty crazy habits, but even when she was naughty, somehow I couldn't help but love her that little bit more. We were a team, a partnership, and I couldn't imagine my life without her. With hand in paw, united we'd stand and divided we'd fall.

Both these souls were changed by each other, as they grew together. A beautiful partnership.

Mandy's story

My cat Gregor is a hero to me because he saved me from two aggressive dogs. I was almost home one day when two dogs started chasing me, barking and growling. I didn't know whether to face them or run, so I tried facing them, thinking they'd back off, but one bit at me, grabbing my bag and tearing it. So I dropped the bag and ran, thinking they'd stay and sniff round my shopping, but they chased me instead. I was running along the front of my garden, panicking, hardly able to breathe, feeling them snapping at my heels, when a little black fireball came snarling and spitting out of the hedge. It was Gregor! He landed right on top of one dog and scratched and bit it. It squealed and turned tail, trying to shake off its tormentor. The other dog didn't know what to do, but when Gregor came stiff-legged towards it, it too ran away. I don't know who owned the dogs, but I went back to get my bag, carrying my brave cat, and I never saw the dogs near my house again!

And Gregor may have come into Mandy's life just for that one moment. That is the sort of sacrifice animals will make for us.

Monika's story

Recently, my doggy 'angel on Earth', Wilma, went to the Rainbow Bridge. She really was my angel on Earth. She was with me almost 11 years after I got her at the age of one and a half. I rescued her from some people who didn't want her anymore. Their loss was my gain. They never realized what they had.

Since the first moment we met, she gave me everything. She never was mine, she loved everyone, but most of all she gave me the will to go forward through all the hard times I've had. She accepted me the way I am, and with her I never had to be an actor. This was very important to me because I never used to get along very well with humans and always had problems with them. My whole life has been a problem. Every time I think things are going well, they go wrong again. I have two other dogs, but they are not Wilma. I love them, but it's not the same. Right now I feel lonely and sad and I don't know how to go forward without my angel on Earth.

This story made me feel very sad, but because Wilma obviously came along specifically to love and heal Monika, I feel she will undoubtedly be back because the job isn't finished.

Cate's story

I work in a care home in Tennessee, mostly at night. This is a time when you have to be extra vigilant, especially in the early hours, as this is often when residents have major health issues.

One night I'd done my rounds and had passed the resident house cat along several corridors. I always think that he's doing his 'rounds', probably prowling for mice, but this time it proved that he was doing a little more than that! In fact, I think he may have been doing the same thing I was! Porter – for that is his name – is a big grey cat of indeterminate breeding, and he's pretty spoiled by the residents, as he loves a cuddle and is very soft-coated. He's a bit overweight, too, but that's only to be expected. Anyway, back to that night. I'd done all the checking and everyone had seemed OK, so I went into the kitchen to get a cup of coffee. Porter suddenly shot into the room and started to weave round my legs, pushing really hard. At first I thought he was just after food, but then I realized he was pushing me away from the food towards the door. He soon realized I was following and he set off, looking back at each turn to make sure I was still following. He led me right back to Mr Peterson's room, where I found he had a heart attack in full flow. It seems to me that Porter sensed this was going to happen and, thanks to him, Mr Peterson's family got to enjoy his company for another three years.

This is the second time I've heard of a cat that did this in a care home. It makes me really sad that many institutions don't allow animals. Think what they and their residents might be missing.

Yvonne's story

Dave was a Rottweiler that weighed in at around 140lbs (63 kilos), but his great size belied his soft nature. When we first got Wednesday, our French rabbit, we trusted Dave with him, and sure enough, Dave just stood looking and then he gently licked Wednesday's ears and lay down. This was the start of Dave's unusual career as a foster-mother.

My daughter Amanda would bring home all kinds of strays to look after, and Dave always did his stuff. He helped bring on three little ducklings struggling to learn to swim by going into the pond and encouraging them onto his back. He'd even gently lift them out if they got into trouble. As the rescues came and went, with everything from a small bunny to an old greyhound, Dave would always make them feel part of his family. He's helped bring up four ducks, three geese, five rabbits, 13 kittens and five puppies – not to mention countless newborn chicks.

Dave was also a PAT dog, which means he was used to provide pet therapy for people in retirement homes and sick children in hospitals. Dave's done a lot to promote the breed and counter-balance its reputation for aggression. Most Rottweilers aren't vicious – they can be very gentle and obedient if they're looked after and trained properly.

Big, powerful breeds often get a bad reputation, but Dave is one of many 'nurse' Rottweilers I've heard of. It seems to be a 'thing' with the breed.

Shania's story

I loved my cat Tommy, but when he left our house and decided to live with an elderly neighbour I couldn't really object as the old man seemed very lonely. Tommy gave him a new lease of life. Four years later the man's condition deteriorated suddenly and he was taken to hospital. We went round to feed Tommy and he showed no signs of wanting to come back with us. The next day, however, he suddenly turned up at ours and took up his old spot. It didn't surprise us when we learned that the old man had died at the exact time Tommy had come home.

Tommy was a nurse cat and he happily returned to his owner once his job with the neighbour was done.

Joanna's story

Dexter the Dalmatian will always be my angel and hero. From the very first minute, we knew he was special. He brought such fun, joy, happiness and love to everyone. Dexter and I had a very special connection, a unique bond, and I was so very proud that such a beautiful, bright and charming boy had chosen us.

I'd never seen such a beauty, and Dexter was thoroughly deserving of our awe. He was extraordinarily intelligent, loyal, gentle and friendly. He was such a beautiful soul, with absolutely stunning looks and good manners. Dexter was a happy, energetic, playful pup (just what you might expect in a Dalmatian), and what fun and absolute joy it was to be with him and watch him grow. He grew more handsome every day, in every way.

Sadly, during his adolescence I sensed something was wrong. After courses of hydrotherapy and osteopathy treatments (and changing vet twice), my husband and I were to hear the dreaded news: our Dexter was a very poorly lad indeed, suffering from very aggressive spondylosis of the spine, for which there was no cure, and he had various joint problems, too.

My heart was breaking, but we tried to keep positive and help our beloved boy. We learned to understand his illness and did everything we could to help him and make him as comfortable as possible. You name it, we explored it, and did it – our Dexter was so deserving.

When I booked a consultation with the wonderful animal communicator Jackie Weaver, I was astounded to hear what our amazing Dexter had to say. Not only were Dexter's symptoms accurately described, but Jackie confirmed what helped his condition, discussed his personality and traits, and also surprised us with Dexter's insights for our future. Accepting of his condition, our beautiful boy had an opportunity to talk, but selflessly he talked about me, how I was going to write a book about him, which would be his legacy, and also told Jackie how I could communicate with animals telepathically, too.

Dexter believed in me when, to be very honest, I had trouble believing in myself. He and Jackie gave me inspiration, and both helped teach me how to communicate with animals – I will always be eternally grateful. My career accomplishments had been gratifying, but not satisfying, up until then. Dexter was my strength and motivation, and we truly helped each other.

It hurt unimaginably to think one day we would say goodbye, but that time came. Even though our Dexter had debilitating health problems, enduring much pain, he remained brave, gentle and loving. He had soldiered on for such a long time, but sadly could not fight forever. My life is richer because of Dexter. Although I miss his special presence more than anything, I know and understand now, more than ever, that he will always be by my side. I believe he's helping me to write these words. My angel is now in heaven.

What a brave dog! And they often do this, going through terrible ordeals to stay with the one they love.

Sallyanne's story

I always played in the woods when I was a kid. I guess it was safer back then, but apart from my parents telling me 'not to talk to strangers' I was pretty much left alone. I was a bit of a loner, too, preferring to play in the fields among the cows, which never troubled me. When I went to the woods I was never scared of the trees, and I was really puzzled that some of the other kids were.

They saw faces in the trunks, they said, bad spirits that would reach out gnarly arms at night and grab them, then drag them down into the earth or into the tree's mouth. I thought they were nuts. I'd even walk in the woods at twilight, and I was never scared – well, not of the trees anyway.

For most of my childhood I had my dog Tallow to keep me company and safe. We grew up together, since my family got her when I was only two years old. What I'm about to tell you happened at a time when Tallow was recovering from a small operation and so couldn't come out with me. I'd given her a hug that morning, told her it was only for a while and gone out alone. I got playing and forgot the time and it was getting dusky as I set off home. I was almost clear of the woods when I started hearing twigs snapping and footsteps. I knew there were some campers nearby, but I wasn't scared of them and I thought it was one of them out rabbiting or something. But after a while the sounds started to come from in front instead of behind me and I knew there was something fishy about this person stalking me, sneaking round to cut me off. When he stepped out of the bushes in front of me I wanted to scream, but nothing would come out. Besides, I was too far away from the houses for anyone to hear me. The man was about 30, scruffy-looking and definitely up to no good. He smiled and walked towards me, herding me into a bramble patch. Soon there would be no escape, I knew that but I couldn't run and was forced to just keep backing away. I felt the thorny bushes at my back and knew I'd run out of space.

'Come on, sweetheart, don't be shy,' the man said.

His words opened my throat and I was able to scream one word, 'Tallow!'

I don't know why I did that, because I knew my little guardian couldn't hear me from where she lay on her bed at home. I reckon the man knew she wasn't around, too, because he smiled again. He reached out his arms, coming to me, and then suddenly a shadow appeared behind him. It flew through the air, and then it and the man went tumbling to the ground. Now it was his turn to yell. It all happened so fast that I can't honestly say for sure what I saw, as I ran past him as fast as I could. I didn't stop running until I crashed through the back door of home and fell to my knees beside Tallow, who greeted me enthusiastically with her wet tongue. I know what it was, though. Somehow my dearest, bravest dog had heard my cry and had sent her shadow to save me. I never, ever told my family what happened, and I never will, but I'm sharing this story with you, Jenny, because I think it's important that people know. I never went into those woods without Tallow again.

I've heard of shadow animals before, although usually they seem to refer to animals who have passed over and returned in this form. This is the only story so far of a dog who transformed into a 'shadow' while she was still alive. If you have heard of another, please let me know!

Tallow's story reminds me a little of my old dog Sally. I never actually saw her as a shadow, but this ability in Tallow might explain something very odd that used to happen with Sally. She was sometimes shut away indoors while I and/or other children played out in the road with a ball. Sally's bed was in the outhouse, which only had one window quite high up, so she couldn't see us. Quite often, almost always in fact, sooner or later the ball would disappear into the thick bushes and hedgerow opposite our house, which was several hundred yards long and about 30 feet thick, and despite our best efforts it would seemingly be lost for good.

Whenever this happened the other children would immediately start calling for Sally, and if I wasn't with them already they'd knock on the door for me to bring her out. Then Sally would simply disappear into the hedge, without any instructions, and always, without fail, reappear in seconds with the ball in her mouth. It was odd because I don't believe she found it by smell, because it could have smelled of any one of a dozen children, and she never hesitated, never sniffed the air, but just went directly to the ball as if she'd not only watched it go into the undergrowth but had also seen exactly where it landed. I have to wonder now, after hearing about Tallow, whether Sally, too, was able to send her shadow where she herself couldn't go.

Carrie's story

Our dog Jonas, a pure white cross-breed, is deaf. He was born deaf so it doesn't bother him. Like people who have a sense that doesn't work properly, his others took over for him. He can sense who's in the room with him as soon as they enter the door, by their scent. I swear he can detect cars coming by the fuel smell, and he's never come close to trying to step in front of one.

Last year, after years of trying, I got pregnant, and my husband and I we were so happy. We knew Jonas would love the baby, but we didn't realize he already had a bond with it. It seemed to us that the pregnancy was going along just fine, but then Jonas started to act in a strange way. He wouldn't leave my side and he kept sniffing my belly. At first it just seemed funny, but then he started to place his paw on it, very gently but insistently, and while he did this he would stare intently at it.

After a while it freaked me out so I went for a check-up. They were very good, not treating me like an over-nervous first-time mom. I couldn't believe it when they discovered I had a slight placental abruption, which if not discovered could have become very serious. They monitored me from then on and our little boy, Jake, was finally safely born.

If Jonas hadn't warned us, we could have lost Jake. When I was in the hospital my husband says he never had to worry in between visits that everything was OK, because he only had to look at our wonderful dog. If he was peaceful and quiet, there would be no problem. Now Jake's here Jonas rarely leaves his side, and we have no worries with such a strong and intuitive guardian on hand.

Did Jonas have a special bond with Carrie or her baby?

Charlotte's story

I have epilepsy, and for a while after I was diagnosed I was still having seizures until they got my medication right. One of the scariest things about it was that I never knew when one would hit me, so I'd be constantly checking out how I was feeling. The slightest thing would make me stop and panic and wonder if one was coming and whether I'd even wake up again if it did. It was a very difficult way to live, always on guard, never able to relax. Life was no fun.

But during this time, my cat Bingo suddenly started going and getting my mom several minutes before I would have an attack. It was still scary, but at least when Bingo was quiet and stayed with me I knew I was OK and wasn't going to be sick. It made those few months a lot easier both for me and for Mom. I was able to stop thinking about getting a seizure all the time. She was my little saviour. And that isn't all.

One day last year Bingo came flying into the house in a type of panic. Mom thought it was about me at first, but I was OK. Bingo scratched at the basement door until Mom opened it, and of course we both followed Bingo down to see what was up. Seconds later a huge tornado hit the house. If we hadn't followed Bingo's lead and been in the basement right then, we might have been killed.

You have to wonder if all cats and dogs (and other pets) have this natural ability, or whether there are just a very few that show an aptitude and so are trained. Or could it be that these particular pets have just this one person they feel empathy so deeply for?

Felicity's story

Tamsin, my gorgeous silver Siamese cat, was a very well-behaved cat all her life. She never had a cross word to say to anyone and she was gentle and kind, even to our son, Dylan, who was a normal, boisterous toddler and not as gentle as we might have preferred! Tamsin did not play favourites. One of her best-loved pastimes was watching our fish in the pond. Now you might think she wanted to catch them and harm them, but that wasn't it. We'd been told when she was a kitten that if you never encouraged cats to play with toys that were furry and squeaked or had feathers, they would grow out of their killer instincts, as they had to be taught them by their mother if they lived with her, or their owners. She was only encouraged to play with rubber toys that made no noise and consequently she never once, to my best knowledge and belief, killed another living thing.

Dylan grew, as children do, and became a nine-year-old schoolboy. Everything had gone well for him at school since he was five, and we'd grown to be complacent that school would never be a problem for him, but at the age of nine, things changed. He became tearful and stopped looking forward to school, but I'm afraid we weren't on the ball and didn't realize he was being bullied. I mean, you don't expect that among such young children! Tamsin had changed, too, she took to mewing at the door whenever Dylan was going to school. He was allowed to go to the bus alone, with all the lectures about being safe from strangers ingrained in his mind, but nobody ever warned him about non-strangers.

It took a couple of weeks before I got the message Tamsin was trying to give me. She got more and more insistent about being allowed out as soon as Dylan left, and finally I gave in. She shot off towards the bus stop which was only 90 metres (100 yards) away. Curious, I followed her. I got to the corner, just out of sight of the bus stop and something made me pause and peer around the corner to see what was going on. Dylan was there and two older boys were pushing him around. I couldn't believe it! I was about to rush over to them and give them a piece of my mind (which would have probably got me into trouble), when a silver streak shot into the fray. I don't know exactly what happened, but there were shrieks of pain and the two older boys took off running, while the 'silver streak' sat down next to Dylan and began to groom herself nonchalantly. I guess Tamsin scratched the boys, or just put the fear of God into them. Whatever happened, they never bullied Dylan again because of his silver-suited, furry guardian angel.

Again – could this cat have been related to Dylan in a past life?

Sam's story

My dog Bennie was the love of my life for 16 years. He was a golden retriever and I honestly believe he saved my life. When he was eight years old, I had cancer. I'd been a very active man all my life, and I was young to have this illness strike me down. I found it hard to talk or move, and after surgery I'd lost some of my faculties and really didn't have the will to go on.

One night I went to sleep having decided that I was going to die. I hadn't told anyone, but I said goodbye to Bennie. I always got cold in bed after the surgery, and that night was no different, but later in the night I was amazed to find that I actually felt warm. At first I thought it was just Bennie – he used to try and warm me up, bless him. But it wasn't just him. Bennie had always been a very playful dog who never grew up, really, and so he had a whole heap of soft toys. Anyway, he'd gone up and down – it must have been at least 20 times, back and forth to the kitchen – and brought every single toy up and put it on me. It seemed to me, as I lay there and cried, that Bennie had brought everything he loved and given it to me in an attempt to pull me out of despair. How could I let him down? And, you know what? It worked. I'll never forget Bennie and what he did for me.

Sometimes we need the stoicism of our pet to see us through a tough time that we wouldn't have got though without them. Bennie was surely a brave and incredible soul to shine such a bright light into his owner's life at such a dark time.

I couldn't end this chapter about cat and dog heroes without including a story about my own dog, Ace, who was a rescue dog and soon became an indispensable member of our family. But she actually saved my life one day. We had some orphan lambs and among them was Teddy, the ram. Teddy was bottle-fed, and at the time we didn't know that hand-reared rams can become very dangerous when they grow up, if not castrated. This was the case with Teddy. What started as playfulness soon developed into full-scale charging and butting, which became steadily worse as he became bigger. We'd already decided to find him another, safer home, when this incident happened. I was walking all three of our dogs around our field one day when Teddy charged me. When an animal of that size hits you at hip height, you tend to fall over, which I did. This left me sprawled on the ground and unable to get to my feet quickly. It was almost fatal, because he charged again, and this time his head was level with mine. His rock-hard skull was about to connect with my head. In the split second that remained, a black blur streaked between us. It was Ace. Despite having been trained never to touch the sheep, she recognized this moment of real danger to me. Without ever drawing blood, she gripped Teddy's ear and turned him away from me. She kept his attention, constantly circling him, all the way back up to the gate, while I hobbled along as fast as I could to safety.

If proof were needed that Ace had saved my life, a few days later we read of a Yorkshire farmer who had actually been killed by a ram in exactly the same way. Without a faithful friend to stop it, the ram had fractured the poor farmer's skull. I had been so lucky that Ace had intervened.

CHAPTER 4

Cats and Dogs That Reincarnate

Even if you believe in people reincarnating, you might doubt that dogs and cats do, too, but you'd be wrong. If you believe animals have souls, then it only stands to reason that they are immortal and can therefore come back in another body to be with us again. My own dog, now called KC, has been back several times. I have been regressed into past lives many times, and she has appeared in many of them.

A general theory that I subscribe to is that a soul begins its existence fragmented into many tiny parts, and that each part starts off as uncoloured by experience. Perhaps, say, as a colony of ants. This puts a whole new perspective on collective intelligence, doesn't it! Then, as each ant dies that soul fragment goes back to the whole and starts to colour it with experience. Next time this same soul, depending on its progress might return as a smaller collective, such as a group of tadpoles. Eventually, this soul will be fragmented into just two of the 'higher' species, such as dogs and cats. When the pair dies the soul then forms one whole and can return as a human.

Where this theory might fall down is it presupposes that when we consider 'higher' species, there is a lot of competition for that title. And, if, as many think, animals are in many ways more connected to their spirituality than humans are, why would they feel the need to 'progress' (if indeed they are progressing) to a human body?

And some animal communicators say that they have encountered pets that have already been people and gone back to being animals. So, like all theories there appear to be exceptions to the rule. Some people feel that we need to have experienced lives as animals first in order to be strong enough to cope with life as humans without totally abandoning our spiritual side. There are many beliefs and many theories, but they all point to animals returning in one form or another.

The comforting thing, if you have lost such a pet, is that every soul keeps their biggest part in heaven at all times. So, no pet, no human, is ever really parted from their root. If a pet (or a child) passes away, one of the worst things is that the one left behind worries that the pet or person they lost will be unhappy and unable to find them. This isn't the case. When a soul reaches heaven, they are immediately reunited with the root of themselves, their owners or their loved ones. We who are left behind are the only ones who suffer, but we must always bear in mind that we are still connected – we must be, because that is a part of our soul residing in heaven and we can never really be parted form our own soul root. No soul is ever 'lost', no soul simply cannot be found.

I hope that if you are someone who adores their cat or dog, you will be one of the lucky ones, like the people who tell their stories below, whose pets have returned to them after they died, in a new body, to be with them again.

Jan's story

Several years ago I was sitting in the lounge one night surrounded by my crystals, which I was sorting out, with my Egyptian Mau cat, Simba, sitting in front of me, watching. I looked up from what I was doing and we both looked at each other, and then something unbelievable happened. I saw Simba's face and body change slowly into a completely different cat. His whole face and body changed and he was much, much thinner in shape, along with having a completely different coloured coat!

I knew straight away he was showing me himself as my cat from a past life. Then his features turned back to Simba's and he just smiled at me! It was an amazing moment, and one I will never forget.

What an intriguing story about a 'changeling' cat!

Judy's story

When I lost my beautiful cat about 12 years ago, it made me feel like never having another one, because I'd loved the one I lost so much. But just over two years ago I decided that I needed to have cats in my life again. I wanted two cats this time so that they could keep each other company. At that time my daughter's cat had three kittens, one boy, one girl and another one that couldn't be determined, so we all decided it was a girl. I wanted two girls, because my old cat had been a male and I didn't want to betray him by having the same sex again. It would have seemed like I was trying to replace him. So when they were six weeks old, I took the two female kittens home and left my daughter with the one boy. My two little girls were very different: one was a short-haired, black-and-white kitten I named Candy, and the other was a long-haired, black Persian-looking girl I named Cleo. I loved them both dearly and they were the greatest of friends, till they got to about six months old, when my 'Cleo' turned into a 'Leo'. He'd got much bigger than his sister and then his male anatomy appeared. I now know he did this to shield the fact he actually was a boy, because he knew I wanted two girls and I wouldn't have taken him if I'd known he was a boy.

He got bigger and bigger and was also a big bully to his sister. That got worse over time, and I always had to watch him when she was around. It also became apparent that he was possessive of me, as he followed me everywhere, and that became a problem. He just wanted me to himself and didn't want to share me with his sister.

Leo had always had a breathing problem since he was born. He was never able to meow or purr, and he coughed a lot. This was due to a valve in his throat not opening and closing properly. The vet told me that they could do an operation to treat his condition, but it didn't always work and could cause other problems. So, as Leo managed very well, I left it. He did not need to 'talk' as I always knew what he wanted and needed. He had the most beautiful, enormous golden eyes and he always knew how to communicate through them.

Leo died just two months ago, at the very young age of two years four months, peacefully and naturally, on our driveway. It was, and still is a traumatic time for me, as I miss him so much. I knew he wouldn't live a long life, but never thought he'd go quite so young. Since his passing I've come to believe that he might have been a reincarnation of the beloved cat we had years before, because he certainly shared a lot of traits with him. I feel that his purpose on this Earth this time round was to bring unconditional love back to me, and he certainly did that very well.

The clincher for me was when I had a spiritual drawing done of Leo, which sits up proud and high in my crystal healing room. The drawing is very accurate of him as an adult cat, and his eyes dominate the picture, just as they did in real life. But you see, the only photo I had taken of him was when 'he' (I thought he was a 'she' then) was only eight weeks old, and the artist never saw it, so to have this A3 portrait of him is quite something. I had only had a spiritual message telling me to take a photo of my cats the week before he died, and I said to myself I must do that sometime, but sadly I never did. If only I had listened to my inner self. Never mind, this is a wonderful portrait and I am forever grateful to the woman who did it. It is done in pastel and, as he was a big black cat, there is much black in it, which accentuates those wonderful, huge golden eyes.

I love this story about Leo and his exceptionally beautiful golden eyes.

Patsy's story

My cat, Sassy, always reminded me of a lion. When I first got her as a little fluffy kitten, she was a gorgeous tawny colour. Her coat was very short and smooth, and people always thought she looked like a small lioness. She grew up into a cat who retained her playfulness, and every birthday I'd buy her a new toy to play with.

She was a bit odd, because she never chased birds. I found that strange. She'd sit and watch them, but it was as if they were beneath her somehow, so she never tried to touch them. She was my best mate for many years, and I always felt that maybe we'd known each other before. When she got ill, aged 17, I was devastated. I knew she was going to die because she kept saying goodbye in various ways. For instance, even though she was weak she brought all her toys to me and laid them in a pile by my chair. I held her in my arms when the vet administered his merciful injection, and my heart broke as she went limp. Once she'd gone, the house seemed so empty. Seventeen years is a long time.

I missed her constantly and so wanted some sort of sign from her, but I got nothing. It was a really bad time for me. One day I felt like I couldn't take it anymore, and when I left the house that day to drive to work I told her in my mind, 'Sassy, you have to give me a sign. If you can still hear me, if you're still somewhere, then show me a new cat that I can't miss on my way to work.' I lived in the countryside, and there were only two cats in the village. So seeing a cat was quite rare, and seeing a different one, next to impossible. As I drove I scanned the hedgerows looking for something, but there wasn't anything. As I turned the final bend into the town I couldn't believe my eyes: a circus was coming to town, and right there on the verge was a huge billboard, and on it a roaring lion. At first I was shocked and delighted, thinking this at last was my sign, but then logic stepped in and I started to doubt – after all, I knew Sassy looked like a lion, but she wasn't one, and the poster must have been put there the previous night, before I'd asked for a sign. I know they say a healthy mind will always look for the logical answer, but this time I wished mine wouldn't! Why couldn't I just believe?

I decided to take further action. I thought I'd go and see a medium, and if she mentioned the lion poster without me telling her about it, then it had to be a real sign from Sassy. I went and, although the reading was good, the medium never mentioned the poster. It was frustrating. In the end I asked her outright, was there a cat trying to get through to me? Her answer left me speechless. She said, 'Not a cat as such, not a domestic one anyway. I'm quite sure there's a mistake here somewhere, but you didn't ever own a lion, did you?' She went on, 'Ah, I see, this is a message from what was a cat. She wants you to know that she's now returned to her true form, what she was in previous lives. Your cat is now a lion again.'

Patsy's story reveals a fascinating message from her cat, confirming that her intuition about Sassy's true lion nature was correct.

Madeleine's story

Our cat Zappa arrived into our lives as a feisty, furry bundle of fluff, and he was with us for 17 eventful years. On the day of his arrival he'd immediately emitted a huge hiss and a spit, belying his diminutive presence, firmly putting the dogs in their place and setting the guidelines as to how he wanted us to live with him. All his life he continued to rule us all with a paw of iron and was considered to have what might politely be called an 'attitude'!

We joked that he carried a government health warning whenever he had to visit the vet, which, over the years, was quite often as he would fight all comers – any cat who dared to venture into his territory – and occasionally his war wounds needed treating. Woe betide anyone who crossed the invisible line he'd drawn while some unsuspecting person was stroking him. We learned to recognize the slightest twitch that would precipitate an attack, which generally resulted in bloodshed. However, we loved him dearly for his character, which commanded the utmost respect.

One day in his seventeenth year he seemed to stumble and lose his balance. His left eye also seemed affected. His condition deteriorated and the vet confirmed he'd had a massive stroke. It was so sad to see that magnificent creature reduced to a shadow of his former self, so we made the only decision we could.

'Please come back to us if you can,' I said as I stared down lovingly at my old, whiskered friend, as his life gently ebbed away.

My son had been just a few months old when Zappa had come to us and had never known a day when the cat had not made his presence felt, so his passing left a huge void in our life. A few months later I visited a friend and told her about Zappa's sad passing, and she said, 'Well, you better have a look in that box over there!' When

I peered in I saw a lovely silver tabby with four kittens. One of the kittens immediately caught my eye, and on subsequent visits he stood out more and more. He had the biggest character, and there was just something about his eyes that seemed familiar. When he was old enough to come home with me, I arrived to pick him up and was greeted by the words, 'I hope you're ready for this – yours is a thug!' I laughed as I saw the kitten gleefully swinging on the ear of a very patient old Springer Spaniel. He then proceeded to perform a wall of death around the kitchen.

When we arrived home the dogs were eager to see what was making all the noise in the basket. I opened the top and the kitten strutted out, tail erect, then proceeded to hiss and spit at the dogs, pee in his litter tray and survey his domain, as if just taking up his place where he'd left off. The dogs, who sense these things, seemed to say, 'Oh, it's you!' They instantly accepted his return, though thankfully he was now a seemingly more gentle incarnation of his previous self! I honestly believe Zappa had been reincarnated to be with us again.

Madeleine's cat just couldn't stay away!

Jo's story

My dog Cassie is a Staffy cross English Bull Terrier, and we adopted her from the local Dog's Trust in Roden, Shropshire, UK. I have clinical depression, but a lot of the time I am OK, and after years of having it I've learned to 'put on a front'. However, Cassie always knows when I'm feeling low, and instead of being her usual bouncy, clumsy self, will approach me very calmly and tenderly. And instead of walking on me like she usually does, she'll sit next to me and just rest her head on my lap.

She is a lot like my old dog, Jess, who we had when I was 11 until I was 22. I was bullied at school, and Jess was also from the Dog's Trust. When I'd get in from school after a bad day, I'd shut myself in my bedroom and have a cry (trying to be as quiet as possible so my brothers didn't hear). But after a minute or so I'd hear scratching at the door, and it would be Jess. She would always come in to comfort me and look after me.

Sometimes I feel that Cassie is a reincarnation of Jessy. They both have the same beautiful brown eyes, and although their personalities are quite different (Jess was very timid and Cassie is very confident), I feel that deep soul connection with both of them. Even when I'm thinking about something, it's as if Cassie will know what I'm thinking. I'll be walking her and thinking, 'Cassie, if you need to poo, please poo here! The next dog poo bin isn't for ages.' And then she'll look at me and, well, you know, do her business.

In Jo's case it seems the eyes really are the windows to the soul.

Billie's story

My Grandad died when I was about 15 years old. I didn't have a dad, so my mom's dad took his place and I loved him so much. He was pretty unforgettable as he had wispy red hair and freckles. After he died I'd cry myself to sleep holding his picture. Something odd happened a few days after his funeral when I was out walking. For no reason I suddenly had this feeling that he was with me, watching over me, and I felt he was trying to say he wouldn't leave me. It was very strong. But I still found it hard to get over losing him.

Then a couple of months later I was out walking again when I heard this whimpering noise in the bushes. I got a little closer, but here in Arizona you do have to be a bit careful of the wildlife, there are some really dangerous snakes out here, so I was wary and didn't go too close at first. But then of course I knew it couldn't be a snake as they don't make that kind of noise, and I could still hear this whimpering and the grass rustling, so I had to look. I gently parted the grass with the tips of my fingers, and saw a sack, and it was wriggling. I snagged it with a stick and pulled it out onto the road. I could see that the animals in the sack were quite small, and that there were two of them, but one wasn't moving at all. I dragged off the string that held the sack closed and gently tipped the sack up, standing as far back as I could.

Two bodies tumbled out. They were puppies! One was lifeless, and I felt so sad at that, but I quickly had my attention taken by the live one! He was really weak and would soon be dead, too, if I didn't do something. I cuddled him in my arms and ran with him to the nearest store to get him some water. Once he had a drink, by me trickling water into his mouth from my fingers, he went to sleep and seemed like he would be OK.

I took the puppy home. There was never any doubt that I'd keep him. We called him Ginger. His coat was wispy and mostly red, and the white bits of fur had red freckles on them. I noticed right away that he reminded me of Grandad, but it wasn't for a couple of days that I really started to get shivers down my spine. We were sitting at the breakfast table and Ginger had grown strong enough to jump, so he clambered onto the spare chair – Grandad's chair, where he'd always sat. Mom and I looked at each other, just amused at that point. He looked so comical, sitting there looking at us expectantly.

Mom felt sorry for him, so she dished him up some eggs, grits and bacon, figuring he'd love it. But Grandad had one thing about him that was odd. Despite raising pigs and eating pork, he had never liked bacon. He just wouldn't eat it. We used to tease him, but he never would. But all dogs love bacon, right? Not this one! He ate the eggs and the grits off the plate in quite a polite way for a dog, then just stared at the bacon in disgust. Ginger never did eat bacon. I never met or heard of another dog that wouldn't, and the only person, apart from vegetarians, I ever met who didn't like bacon was Grandad.

Could Billie's Grandad have come back as a dog? It's one way to return to the same family without having to go through all the growing up humans have to do.

Joy's story

Ginger was the gentlest, most loving cat on the planet. We had him for 15 glorious years, but the day came when he became ill and we had to have him put to sleep. We had him cremated and I put Ginger's remains in my bedroom with a picture of him on the top.

A year passed, but I couldn't bear the thought of trying to replace Ginger because he had been so special. Unbeknown to me, my children went to the RSPCA and they came home with a tortoiseshell female. She was tiny, with massive ears and big eyes. She also had one ginger paw, and I remember thinking that Ginger must have sent her to us. My husband named her Poppy. She was a wild little minx and very mischievous. As she matured she was always at my side. I came to think that she was my soulmate.

Poppy reached the age of 14, and I could see that she was slowing down and looking quite old. One night at about 2 a.m. I heard a piercing scream coming from the dining room. I rushed down and there was Poppy, in the throes of a heart attack. The vet came, but there was nothing he could do. We had Poppy cremated the next day and I've got her ashes in my bedroom next to Ginger's. The night of the cremation, Poppy appeared to me. She looked at me as if to say, 'Look, I'm OK,' and then she ran off. I do hope to see her again.

This story about another Ginger – this time a cat – and his successor Poppy, shows how some pets continue the bond with their special human by coming back in a new body or in spirit.

CHAPTER 5

Ghost Pets

I know I've lost pets that I have felt I couldn't live without, and I know lots of other people have too. Many of the people who pick up this book will have felt the terrible loss that all pet lovers know. It's one of the great sorrows in life that cats and dogs don't live as long as people. But I've found it very comforting at times to feel that familiar brush of a nose or swish of a tail and have even seen a fleeting shadow or felt an animal jump on the bed as they always used to in life, after they've passed. So, I'm not surprised that so many people also experience a re-visit from their dog or cat after it has passed over. Our dogs and cats empathize so much with us when they're alive that it's no wonder they sometimes hang around and try their hardest to make us feel better. There's a beautiful, anonymous poem called Rainbow Bridge, which has comforted many, and speaks of a place where pets wait for their owners to join them:

Just this side of heaven is a place called Rainbow Bridge.

When an animal dies that has been especially close to someone here, that pet goes to Rainbow Bridge. There are meadows and hills for all of our special friends so they can run and play together. There is plenty of food, water and sunshine, and our friends are warm and comfortable.

All the animals who had been ill and old are restored to health and vigour. Those who were hurt or maimed are made whole and strong again, just as we remember them in our dreams of days and times gone by. The animals are happy and content, except for one small thing; they each miss someone very special to them, who had to be left behind.

They all run and play together, but the day comes when one suddenly stops and looks into the distance. His bright eyes are intent. His eager body quivers. Suddenly he begins to run from the group, flying over the green grass, his legs carrying him faster and faster.

You have been spotted, and when you and your special friend finally meet, you cling together in joyous reunion, never to be parted again. The happy kisses rain upon your face; your hands again caress the beloved head, and you look once more into the trusting eyes of your pet, so long gone from your life but never absent from your heart.

Then you cross Rainbow Bridge together.

Mary Ellen's story

I really should have known better than to buy red paint the same day I took home a stray kitten: I mean the two things don't really go together, do they! My excuse is that I had already bought the paint and was on my way home to do a feature wall in my big room, when our paths crossed. There was a drainage ditch next to the road and it was full of water after the storms that had thundered through during the night. As I flashed past one stretch of water I caught a glimpse of something bobbing about on the surface and although I couldn't have said what it was, something subliminal must have kicked in, because it made me brake and reverse back to it. There, floating precariously on the water, perched on a square of polystyrene, was a bedraggled kitten. As she rushed past me on the current I heard her shout out as if to get my attention. She was a tabby, nothing special to look at, except she was outstanding in her obvious tenacity to cling to life. I ran alongside, overtaking her, and knelt down as she caught me up, and finally managed to fish out the polystyrene, kitten and all. She had her tiny claws imbedded into it and didn't let go her hold on it until I had both hands around her. But right then she started to purr. The slightest touch of a human hand always made her do that for her whole life. I called her Bobble, because of how I found her bobbing along like a cork.

My house was rented and the landlord just about allowed one pet, thank goodness. He also allowed tenants (and I was a long-term one) to redecorate, hence the paint. I'm sure you can imagine what happened later that day. Yes, one new and mischievous kitten, one open pot of red paint, and a lovely set of paw prints on the carpet! I had to replace it and nearly regretted by new friend's arrival, but it was soon forgotten.

Bobble grew up into a fantastic little soul. She used to accompany me on my job, which often involved talking to kids who were in care and had often been abused in some way. No matter what their reaction or how they tried to shut down to me, Bobble would climb determinedly up onto their laps, onto their chests and would stare solemnly into their eyes for a minute, as close as she could get. Then she would start to purr. It rarely failed to bring the kid out of their shell. She loved travelling in the car with me and I loved her so much. Of course, eventually the sad day came – though I tried not to let it – when Bobble slipped away from me. She was 16 years old by then and we'd had such a wonderful time together. I thought my life would never be healed and that I'd be heartbroken forever. I was sure I would never find another companion like her.

I took to just sitting around, moping, waiting for the grief to ease, waiting for the hole in my heart to heal, but it didn't. I kept thinking she was so special! Surely, she wasn't going to just leave me without some sort of sign that she was OK?

I read a book called 'Pets Have Souls Too', and envied the people who had written in about their pets coming back in ghostly form to make them feel better. I waited and waited to feel Bobble's nose in my hand, or her tail whisking across my leg, or to see a shadowy form scooting around the house, but nothing… until one rainy night. It's not what you're thinking. None of the above happened. But that night I dreamed of her and the first day I brought her home and the paint. Now bearing in mind that I hadn't just tried to clean the carpet she paddled on with paint on her feet – she'd done far too good a job of it for that – but had bought an entire new carpet, you can imagine my face when, in the morning, I came into the big room to see dead centre in the floor, one perfect, red, paw print! I was absolutely ecstatic! I vowed right then, never to clean this one off or replace it, no matter what the landlord said. In fact, I covered it with a rug because I didn't know if it was actually paint or something less durable, and I didn't want it to get worn off. Anytime I felt down and alone without my buddy, I could just whip up the rug and there it would be. If I ever move from here I will cut out that bit of carpet and take it with me – even if I have to replace the whole thing!

That's not quite the end of the story. The day of the paw print's appearance, someone at work brought in a kitten, looking for a home for it. It was black and white with a big pink nose, just like the bobble on a bobble hat. The rest as they say is history…

What sense of humour Mary-Ellen's cat's soul had!

Crystal George's story
(about a rather larger cat than usual)

I was brought up among game farms and was quite used to seeing big cats. They never scared me because I always knew how to act around them. There was just one time that really freaked me out. I was visiting a friend's holiday complex and got there a bit earlier than she said to, so I was just hanging around until she got back from town. I went down, very quietly, to the water hole to see if anything was around, making sure I was upwind of the water. There were some zebras drinking, and that was about it. I sat down in the brush hide to watch. After a while I saw a shadow slinking through the trees. I squinted, trying to make it out. It looked like a lion. I was thinking this was totally fantastic, because I knew how long Patty's family (who owned the park) had been wanting their own lion. Over here, mad as it sounds, people who have fenced off some of the wilderness often have to buy animals to put in it. All the wildlife is actually owned by someone around here. Patty's mum and dad hadn't been able to afford a lion yet, so I was really pleased to see that obviously they had now.

The lion, still in the shadows, seemed to be creeping up on the zebras. That put me in a difficult spot. It's an unwritten law that you don't step in and stop a lion (or any other predator) hunting. They have to live, after all, and it's up to the owners to make sure there are enough prey animals to maintain a balance. If you wanted lions, you had to be willing to sacrifice the odd zebra. I hated to see it, though. Lions are actually pretty kind the way they kill. They don't savage their prey like some big cats; they grab hold of the nose and suffocate them. But still I didn't like to see it. I looked around and no one was watching. The lion was sneaking up on the cutest baby zebra and I thought I'd just save this one. It was only a baby, after all. I knew that if I made a lot of movement the zebras would run off, so I came out of the hide and started jumping up and down, pretty confident that the lion, who was the other side of the water hole, wouldn't even think of coming after me – I was too close to the cabins.

It worked perfectly and the zebras ran for the hills. But the funny thing was, the lion took no notice either of them or of me. He continued his prowl as if the zebras were still there. I couldn't understand what was going on. By now I could see he was a beautiful specimen, healthy and well-fed, so Patty's family had done well to get him. Then I could see that the lion was about to spring, but on nothing! He leapt and vanished – all that was left was a cloud of dust. I couldn't believe my eyes. I must have blinked or something and missed him, I thought. Lions can move really fast, but still, the nearest cover had been yards away.

At that moment Patty came walking up behind me. I told her how pleased I was that she'd got a lion at last. She looked puzzled, 'What lion?' she asked, 'We won't be getting one for months yet.'

That story is, so far, the only ghost animal story to come to me out of Africa.

Margaret's story

Turner, was a feral cat I rescued and tamed. When I got him he was shy and scared, but as the years with us passed he became more and more confident. In the end he was a very loving cat, but I started to worry about him because it was impossible to keep him from wandering, and he wasn't above taking on the local dogs either. He would always come home in the morning to eat, sleep and play, then he'd go out for a while, always coming back in the evening and spending some time with us, snuggled up on the couch before going out again for the night. When he was home he turned into the gentlest of creatures. He would look after my toddler son and sit and watch my elder son do his homework. Chester, my 12-year-old son, used to say that he couldn't concentrate if Turner wasn't there, and he swore the cat was helping him somehow. On the other hand, Turner would sometimes stalk strangers who came up the path, and quite scared one or two of them because he was a large cat. We honestly thought he was as good as a dog when it came to guarding the house.

One day my worst fears were realized when Turner didn't come home in the morning, and eventually he was brought to me by a neighbour who'd found him dead in the street. His injuries could have been from a car or from an attack by a pack of dogs. Anyway, we buried him in our backyard with great sadness and ceremony. That night I distinctly heard feather-like but audible paws padding along the wooden floors of our hallway, although I had no other animals at the time. I could only think it was a stray that had somehow got in. I felt this cat bounce up onto the bed and walk up to my face, but when I opened my eyes, there was nothing there. I sat up – the door was closed tight. I thought I must have been dreaming, but another day when I was watching TV stretched out on the couch, I felt a cat nuzzle up to my feet, just like Turner used to do. This time I was awake, so I knew I wasn't dreaming.

Eventually I told Chester what had happened. I thought he'd laugh, or be scared, even, but all he said was, 'Mom, I heard a cat purring every night for a week after Turner died, right by my ear while I was doing my homework.'

I just sat with my mouth open, and then asked, 'Is it still happening?'

'No,' said Chester sadly, 'I guess from now on I have to do my own thinking.'

Even though Turner only came back briefly this time, I have a feeling he will return again one day in Chester's future.

Garret's story

Blue and Stormy had been born to a pair of alley cats. The two were never apart in life and ended up being very good 'watch cats'. They would take turns, and if you stayed up you could watch 'the changing of the guard'. Four years later we added a third cat, Spot. Blue saw to her training and she joined the 'patrol'.

After my retirement from the Navy, we moved to Austin, Texas. Blue, now nearing 13 years old, was in poor health by then and we had to hand-feed her liquids and super-soft foods, but she still kept up her watch. I would get up in the mornings to get the kids ready for school and check on her, she would meow at me and then sleep, knowing that she had been 'relieved from duty'.

One morning I went to check on her, and as I reached for her she gave a very loud, strong meow! I said, 'Well, you're feeling good…' but as I touched her I realized that she had passed during the night, for she was cold and stiff to the touch. I am confident that she 'remained on watch' until I relieved her, and that she said goodbye to me.

Fast forward to an evening in November four years later. Blue's sister Stormy (now 16 years old) is greying and moving slowly and stiffly. I'm in my bedroom and I hear a loud 'MEOW!' from the hallway. This did not sound like either Stormy or Spot, but like Blue... I then heard Stormy meow, as if in answer to her sister. Then she meowed three more times: one sounded like she was facing my closed bedroom door, and then one for each for the other two bedrooms... My son told me later that he'd seen Stormy exit the hallway and climb into the cat carrier, as if she expected to go on a trip. An hour later she was gone. She and Blue are back together as they were in life.

Goosebumps, that's the only word I need to say.

Suki's story

Family and friends were worried that Ben, our beloved dog, might inadvertently harm my newborn twins, but he was always wonderful with them. He cried when they cried and comforted them.

One day Ben suffered a stroke. His hind legs were paralysed. He couldn't bark, couldn't wag his tail, and lost bowel and bladder control. The vets told us to put him down. But I couldn't do it.

I took Ben swimming three times a week, did physio with him and showered him with love and care. Months later, suddenly he was standing up. I cried with happiness. Eventually Ben was able to walk again, though he was never able to run. He also regained all his other functions. The vets were amazed.

Years later, one evening Ben couldn't put his front paw down. The vet gave him a painkiller injection, but that weekend Ben kept sitting and barking at me, as if calling me to be with him. I was in an armchair and Ben was on his bed near my feet. I went to him, hugged him and said a few comforting words, then went back to my armchair. He barked again and I went to him again. I joked with him, saying I couldn't keep doing this. The next morning I was horrified to find he'd started bleeding in the night.

Ben had a tumour and bone cancer, which was spreading very fast. We had no choice but to put him to sleep. He went peacefully, looking at all of us. We all cried and my eyes got filled with this light. I think it was maybe Ben's spirit. We planted a blossom tree in the garden with a memorial stone. I was woken up in the middle of the night by Ben's scent. I remember smiling and going back to sleep happy.

This was a difficult end for this dog, but I have a feeling he knew what he was doing.

Delilah's story

My husband, Martin, and I run a company called Pet Paws offering services such as pet-sitting, cat and dog boarding and walking, and we also run an animal ambulance. Sadly, this often involves taking an animal for its last journey to the vet.

Toby was an old dog, 14 years old. He was blind and unable to use his legs. He belonged to an old woman who lived alone with him, and the bond of love was very strong between them. We had taken Toby to the vet twice before for her, each time thinking it would be the last time for him. Both times, happily, we were able to take him back home to his owner. This time there was no hope. The vet said his legs would not recover and that the kindest thing to do would be to put him to sleep. As we're Reiki healers, we gave Toby some Reiki, not to heal but to help him on his journey. We left Toby with the vet, knowing he would see the old dog gently away, and with heavy hearts started to make our way back home in the ambulance.

We'd travelled about a mile down the road and were at some traffic lights. While sitting there waiting for the lights to go green, we suddenly looked at one another in amazement, because we could both clearly hear a dog whimpering in the back of the ambulance. Then the whimpering turned to a panting noise. Although we both knew that there were no dogs in the van, we both turned to look in the back, because we could both clearly hear that there was a dog back there. The noise of the dog whimpering and panting lasted until the lights turned green, and we started to move off with the traffic. Then they stopped.

I think Toby was passing over just as we got to the lights and was crying because he wanted to travel back in the ambulance to his owner, just as he had done twice before.

I'm sure Toby's owner was very comforted when they told her what had happened and that Toby still existed somewhere at Rainbow Bridge and would be waiting for her one day.

Joan's story

I was looking after my friend's dog, Sam, while she visited her husband in hospital. Sam liked to have company. He wasn't naughty or anything, he just got grumpy if left alone too long. He was a worrier! This ended up going on for two weeks during which I got to know Sam pretty well.

I soon realized that whenever he got excited and started jumping at the window, his owner would pull up outside within 10 minutes. Sam couldn't have heard the car I don't think as they lived on an

A road and the noise was too loud in general for him to pick one car out 10 minutes away. Also, the times varied enormously, as she often had to stay with her husband for longer than expected as he had various treatments and tests.

But that apparent telepathic link wasn't all. One day when I was there he started whining at an apparently empty corner of the room. It totally freaked me out and I stared at the corner but couldn't see anything. Then on the third or fourth day I saw a shape in the corner. It was a cat! My neighbour was not a cat person, so I immediately thought it couldn't be hers, and then it hit me, why could I suddenly see it? It couldn't be real because on the previous few days it hadn't been visible. Then I got goose bumps as I realized I could see the wall through it. It was an almost white cat, with mink-coloured paws, face and tail. I could see its eyes glowing with bright blue light, and then it vanished.

I didn't know whether to tell my neighbour or not, as I didn't want to scare her, but when she came home it was with terrible news. Her husband had died while she was with him. I shook inside as I realized the time he died was the same time as the cat had appeared. What should I do? Might it comfort her? It must mean something, but would it be insensitive to mention it? I decided to wait. She was sad about her husband, but it had been expected really. Still I thought, she might laugh, or even get angry, so I left it.

One day she was reminiscing about her husband, and one of the things she said was that it was strange how they had got together and stayed together as they had completely different tastes in most things. For instance she said, 'He was a cat person, and I am a dog person. So we shouldn't really have got along.' I asked her if they'd ever had a cat, and she said they hadn't, which stopped where my thoughts had been going. But then she said, 'He did have a cat when he was a boy though. He said when she died he'd never get another, as she'd been too special, and he never did. He said she was the most beautiful cat he'd ever seen. She was white with beige paws, face, ears and tail, and brilliant blue eyes.'

I have no doubt that his cat came back for him. But how could I explain why it had come to their house, where it had never been, and why didn't it appear next to him at the hospital instead of with me? I have a strong suspicion it was something to do with Sam. I'd be mortified if I told her and it upset her. Maybe one day, I will tell my neighbour and see what she says.

I really hope that Joan finds a way to tell her neighbour. I'm sure it will be the right thing to do.

Charlotte's story

Chloe was always my dog, right from when I was young until she was 14. I lived with her until I got married, and at the point I am writing about she hadn't yet ever been to the new home that I shared with my husband. One night I had an awful dream of seeing Chloe standing outside the French doors, even though she'd never been there for real. In the dream I rushed out and threw my arms around her neck. I was crying because I thought her visit meant she was dead. I buried my face in her coat, and I could feel and smell her. I could feel her breath. I begged her, 'No! No! You can't go! You can't die! Don't go!' I was thinking these feelings so hard and desperately that it hurt. Finally, I let go of her and she ran off round the corner of the house.

When I woke up, right away I sent a text to my mum, fearfully dreading the reply to my question about whether Chloe had passed. My mum reassured me that my dog was fine. But two days I had to rush home when I got a call to say that Chloe had gone outside and suddenly was too weak to get back in, too weak even to move. My mum called the vet in and when I got there Chloe was put to sleep, sitting between my legs on the floor, as she always used to when she was younger. I honestly believe that the night she came to see me she was ready to go, but because I cried and was so desperate for her to stay, she somehow held on a bit longer. I'm very thankful that I must have meant that much to her that she would do that, and I still remember the whole thing clearly, even now.

How lovely that Chloe made sure Charlotte had some warning of her passing, and enough to make sure she was ready to be with her friend at the end.

CHAPTER 6

Dogs and Cats That Communicate

I've had some truly amazing experiences with animal communicators, none more so than with Jackie Weaver, who is well-known for working with celebrities' pets. She once asked to come and visit me and my dog KC, to include the encounter in her first book.

It was a remarkable experience. I am of course able to communicate with KC on a day-to-day basis, but sometimes, as with all readings of a psychic nature, if you're too close to the subject it's hard to know exactly how much your personal knowledge impinges on what you feel when it comes to the important questions, but I was staggered with what Jackie managed to coax out of her. She had no knowledge at all of KC, so everything was clear and simple and not to be misunderstood or over-interpreted. When Jackie came along and proved conclusively that she could indeed 'talk' to KC, it was great confirmation of what I already knew.

Jackie was able to describe KC's favourite walk, the exact terms of endearment I use on a daily basis and pinpoint precisely the seat of KC's previous lameness. Now all of these things could, to the sceptic, be extremely good guesses, so when Jackie came up with the information I share below, I was very pleased and I defy anyone to doubt them.

She told us that KC felt she had extra sensitive hearing, which often made her cower away from noisy things, as they hurt her ears. She told me KC wasn't afraid of cars themselves, but of the racket they made, which made noise at a pitch her ears could not tolerate. This was quite true. She also told me that when KC was very content or pleased she made a noise in her throat. Again, this was quite right – we often called it her doggy purr. She then asked KC if I ever did anything that had impressed her, the thought of which made me laugh. As if! And if there was anything I did she thought I was good at. KC 'told' her in thought that she'd been quite impressed watching me take a lot of trouble drawing some specific shapes and details on something she described as two circles that looked a bit like a piece of machinery, all the while accompanied by a quiet 'buzzy' noise. What Jackie did not know, could not possibly know, is that the day before I'd spent a couple of hours on the computer designing a CD cover for my good friend Madeleine Walker (Jackie does not know her, either). The design was based around a double circle, with various intricate, symmetrical shapes such as hearts, stars and moons around it and in it. It did take a lot of time and effort as it was the first time I'd attempted such a thing. KC had sat and watched the whole time and listened to the constant 'buzz' of my computer's whirring brain. To me these personal and unique messages were indisputable proof that Jackie was able to communicate with my dog.

The fact that people can communicate with animals adds weight to the evidence of them having souls. How could a being communicate on a mental and energetic level if they were not connected to us? We believe we have souls, and so it follows that dogs and cats (and other animals) do, too.

Here are some more examples of the amazing people, both professional (in these instances I've included website details in case you're interested in discovering more about them) and amateur, who have connected with dogs and cats.

Linda Lowey

www.talkingwithanimals.co.uk

As a child growing up I loved animals and one of my dearest desires was to be among horses. I can always remember my mother warning me not to go up to strange dogs because they may not be very nice. But that thought had never crossed my mind – I felt compelled to say hello and make a connection.

On reflection, what my mother was doing was protecting me from harm, but on a deeper level she was imposing her fears upon me, fears that I had not felt, for my connection with the animals was one that my mother was not experiencing. She was having her own experience. This was a learning curve for me, to trust in my own instincts and to believe in myself. What I am feeling, sensing and thinking may not be the same as others but it does not mean I am wrong. So I quickly learned that people unintentionally impose unnecessary fears and restrict that intuitive spontaneity we all have as children.

During childhood I grew up in a family that liked the idea of animals, but never truly embraced what really having animals was meant to be like. So, our pets very much had their place and lived in some very unsuitable environments, although they were much loved. There was Bruce, who was a toy poodle. Bruce was a snappy little thing and for this reason it was felt that he needed a home without children, one on one, so we lost him to a new home. Then a journey to Battersea Dogs Home brought Prince into our lives. He was a Welsh border collie and, unbeknown to my parents, an animal that needed a lot of exercise and time in grooming. This meant that, with our family's busy lifestyle, the true bond of animal and owners never really happened. Prince told us in the only way he knew how that he was unhappy: by leaving his mark in the kitchen where he was kept. But I remember Prince as being happiest when we were very active at the park going down the slides and jumping onto the roundabout. He had so much love to give but none of us knew how to listen.

Then there were several cats that passed through, including Sooty – who was, as you are probably imagining, a black tom cat. He was quite big, with a flick of white under his chin, and if there was an old cat soul in existence, then that would be Sooty. He seemed to know when we were coming home and was always there to greet each and every one of us. This was just one thing that was most lovable about him. He was such a social, healing animal and he gave pleasure to so many patients at the doctor's surgery that eventually he became the surgery cat, until he passed over at the age of 18.

Many events took place in my life, the same as happens in most people's lives: getting married, having a son, separation from husband and subsequent divorce, before another pet arrived. When my son was aged three, I felt it was important to introduce him to keeping animals and see the care that was really needed. By this time I knew a lot about handling and caring for animals, and had learned from my family's early mistakes. I'd come to understand the bond there should be between a pet and its owner. I felt it was very important to pass this knowledge on to my son so that he, too, would love animals as I did, and understand that sense of being at one with them.

My son and I chose a little kitten together, but sadly it died within a week of feline enteritis. This was at least an example to my son of the irresponsibility of some humans. If people are going to allow their cats to mate then they should make sure they are safe to mate. The tragedy of the kitten's death happened one night while I was at work, and my son had been collected from the day nursery by his grandad. As they walked into the kitchen they discovered the little one already in a very poor state.

In time we gave a home to two black kittens and chose to call them Bonnie and Clyde. Clyde was such a big cat and an adventurer, always out exploring, but one night he never came home and from that moment Bonnie was never far from sight. She was almost a house cat, but she was quite dominant, knowing how to let my son know when he'd gone too far, but it was always only just enough to let him know. She had a heart of gold and gave unlimited love and affection as well as making us laugh. You would find her sleeping in the oddest of places and the smallest of containers, wrapped around the top of a plant pot or tucked in a toy box. Her typing skills on the computer far exceeded my own, and to write with a pen was just fun. I could almost hear her laughter as she frustrated my progress. What a delight to know that personality – and to have great memories of all our much-loved pets.

Shortly after my father passed, and by the time my son was 14, a little Maltese Terrier came into our lives and we called her Pepper. She was funny and so small, this ball of white fluff that could squeeze under furniture and follow you everywhere. Pepper was like the little girl I had never had. She brought immeasurable joy and, as the bond between us grew, the trust was without question. She knew that if I told her something was for her own good, it truly was and she responded as if she knew what every word meant. So often she'd know what I was doing before I knew myself, and her patience and loyalty were infinite. She played often with her sister, who lived nearby, going for walks and runs, barking for play, to warn and for attention. Her sister used to tell tales on her. Pepper was a laid-back, relaxed, cool-dude type of dog and her sister was highly strung and somewhat constipated with stress. If Pepper, for whatever reason, couldn't get out of the door, her sister used to go up to her owner and pull on her leg until she followed her downstairs or from the other side of the house, to let her know the door wasn't open for Pepper. Together they were amazing and bought tears of joy to us so often. As I remember this now, the tears touch my eyes for the loss of that most beautiful of friendships, based on love, loyalty and trust. Pepper may have been stuck in a four-legged body, but she was as human as you and me, with eyes that you became lost in as the love shone through.

Our life together was a 13-year betrothal of constant companionship and togetherness. She passed early on a Sunday morning, which was a day like any other. There were no signs that she would be leaving me that day – none at all – quite the opposite, for I knew when she was unwell and there were no signs. Almost to the day the previous year, Pepper had become very ill and I'd had to take her to the vet. I'd asked them what was wrong with her, and none of what they did seemed to help – in fact, the medication made her worse. So, I took faith and believed in myself, and stopped all medication. I began to treat her naturally through vitamins and diet, and the minute I did so she seemed to rally. I researched foods and supplements, finding out what she needed to maintain a balanced and healthy life with all the necessary nutrients. Only occasionally did she taste pre-packed or manufactured food again. She enjoyed a wide variety of breakfasts and dinners, eating as well as any human. It kept her going for another year, a year I would always be grateful for, because that last year together was possibly the most connected one I could ever have hoped for.

Pepper was a teacher in my life in many ways, and she still remains so in the spirit world. It was she that taught me the ground-breaking knowledge that we can truly communicate with animals and I, in turn, try to pass this on today. However, the shock of her going was enough to bear for a few days. I lit a candle for her and laid her to rest in her bed, which she'd loved dearly. I rang her sister's mum, and of course my son, so they could say goodbye. It was the weekend so it felt reasonable to keep her body until the following Tuesday, making Monday the time to make arrangements and prepare her physical body. This enabled her soul the time to transit into the spirit world. Her passing was so sudden it felt right to allow time and space, as we know it.

It turned out that Pepper had died because of an aneurysm, which is a small clot of blood, and within seconds she was gone. If there were any one way to pass from this life to another, this would have to be one of the kindest ways. After Tuesday it was so quiet. All normality had been disrupted. There were no demands like feeding and walking Pepper, no food to prepare, no doors to open, no friend by my side, and the tears flowed slowly as I tried to understand – why? Why was it so important for Pepper to leave now? When I asked the question in my mind, the answer came that I had always put her first and it was now my time to put myself first and move forward in life. Here was my Pepper talking with me from the spirit world, and as usual she was right. Life had become very restricted, working and breathing life from home. When we did go out she was the first to be said hello to and then me; when we walked she was first to greet all people and the first to warn me of bad people. In some ways she knew that she stood between me and the outside world. She continues to guide me and comfort me. When I teach, she teaches with me, and she has become the most natural animal to communicate with and learn from. I know now I have not lost her at all because she walks within me and with me wherever my path leads, and she is still leading – no one else sees her, that's all. But I believe, and that's all that matters.

Teaching animal communication to others is when we work together most, to bring about the tremendous rewards and realizations, so that people can experience that same belief for themselves. I want to teach that we can all communicate with animals without exception. Our faith and willingness to believe it is possible is the key. The workshops I run are aimed at helping people realize this, so that they know and believe that they too can communicate with animals without question. They come to know that, with practice, they can develop the skill to truly engage with the animal they're communicating with, which can then provide healing on many levels. I'm able to have a three-way conversation with the owner and the animal, with myself as the pivotal connector, and I aim to teach this to others. I am also able to teach people to locate a lost animal, remembering that the animal is only lost as far as the owner's concerned, and it's not until you communicate with the animal that you can know if they are truly lost or have just left home by choice.

Animal communication is an opportunity to relate to the animal world and understand their mental, physical, emotional and spiritual being; what it is they want from us – what their purpose is in our lives. It's when we see the balance of control in this way that we are able to truly touch the soul of an animal as an equal.

Oephebia

www.animalscantalk2me.com

You might wonder, if you ask me to do a healing session on your pet, what you'll be expected to do, if anything. The answer is very little. During a distant healing session with me your pet can be allowed to do whatever they want because I'll be working on their energy field, and their physical place in space won't impact on that.

During a hands-on healing session, your pet may investigate my hands or push their body into my hands or stay away from me and observe me. There are no rules; your pet will be in charge of the session and I'll work with them with my hands on their body or I'll just be with them, even if they're sitting away from me. Your pet might go into a deep state of relaxation or even sleep. Be assured that all animals are treated with love, compassion and respect.

As an animal communicator and healer, I often come across animals that are aware that they're on the last leg of their journey on Earth, animals that have a mission in this life, and animals requesting to be helped to pass over. These are just some of the stories of these amazing animals.

One communication I did a few years ago, with a cat called Barnaby, illustrates how much animals are aware of their own mortality and the purpose of their lives.

Barnaby's guardian contacted me, as she wanted to know how he was feeling. After a little chit-chat about him, his life, his favourite activities, food, etc. ... he then conveyed to me as a matter of fact that his time on Earth was coming to an end. He simply made me aware of that fact, without drama and without fuss. To me he was a kind of Bob Marley of the feline world: cool and laid back.

He was very chilled out about an event he knew was coming. The wisdom and acceptance emanating from him was mind-blowing, and I could not believe my ears. It was highly unexpected to have an animal telling an animal communicator about their imminent passing without being prompted. He just dropped it in the conversation, as you do.

He explained to me that he was quite ready to undertake his last journey, that he had had a wonderful and exciting life with his guardian and that his body was growing old and weary. At this point Barnaby was in good health, with only a problem with his gums. The vet had found nothing wrong with him and he was enjoying a good life, being mischievous and arguing with his sister, a fiery ginger cat.

Five months later, his guardian contacted me again as she was worried that he was declining but, again, the vet couldn't find anything wrong with him. As soon as I connected with Barnaby, I could feel that his energies were running low and that indeed his life-force was slowly decreasing. He was happy to communicate with me and told me that the end was drawing closer.

He told me that his purpose in life had been to look after his guardian and to make her unwind. This made me smile, as his guardian is someone who's always on the go, very busy and sociable and rarely quiet and relaxed. He made sure she took some time to stroke him or to play with him; he greeted her when she came back home; he slept on her bed and her pillow, to be close to her. In all, he was her little shadow. To him his mission was simple but powerful and he felt he'd accomplished it. Again, serenity and peace were all around him, and he was very philosophical about his own demise. He conveyed that he would go on his own when the final hour was upon him, and little did I know what he really meant by that.

A few months later his guardian contacted me again, and I could sense in her voice that something was wrong. Barnaby had disappeared without trace. Baffled, I communicated with Barnaby straight away, and the answers came back clear to me. Barnaby had gone somewhere reclusive to inhale his last breath on Earth. His body was somewhere in the neighbourhood, but his soul had ascended and was long gone from his forlorn body. He gave me a specific message for his guardian and expressed that his passing was peaceful and as he had wanted. His guardian received the message with a heavy heart, and said she'd known deep down that he was gone. I'll never forget this communication, as it made me understand that some animals have psychic abilities, know about their own future and are very conscious of their mortality.

Here's another extraordinary and remarkable story about the soul of an animal.

I was asked to do some healing sessions on a wonderful little dog called Zephyr. She was a very cute little madam who had a problem with breathing. Often during healing, I leave the communication channel open to let the animal commune with me if they want to. Zephyr knew that and took advantage of the offer. She conveyed a few things about what had been done to her sleeping arrangements in recent times and displayed her disapproval. When I told her guardian about this, the woman was stunned, especially by Zephyr's request to return to the original arrangements, which made a load of sense. She did this and, hey presto, Zephyr displayed her satisfaction.

The healing sessions went well and Zephyr's breathing problem started to abate, and even disappeared altogether. She asked for a few things to improve her health (she was in her twilight years), which duly happened after a few simple adjustments to her diet, and she enjoyed her walks and life.

A few months after the healing, her guardian contacted me and told me that Zephyr had passed away unexpectedly in their garden. She was inconsolable and I must admit that I, too, was sobbing on the telephone, as this little dog had so much charisma and character. I was very fond of her.

A few days later, she phoned again and told me that Zephyr had appeared to her in the front room, her body restored to full health, her coat shining, looking like a young dog again. The apparition lasted for a few minutes and the woman said that Zephyr told her not to grieve for her as she was happy now and that soon enough she'd be back on Earth. The woman was very happy to have seen her dog one last time and she wanted my opinion on the matter. I told her that I believe she did indeed see her dog and that possibly another puppy would come into her life very soon that would remind her of Zephyr. Sure enough, two months later the woman contacted me again and told me that she'd adopted a new puppy. She sent me some photos to have a look at and I could feel Zephyr's spirit around this puppy. The woman confirmed that the new puppy displayed loads of the character traits and likes and dislikes that Zephyr had had.

I found this curious, as they were not the same breed at all, so these similarities could not be classified as breed characteristics. Very strange indeed, but I am happy to know that Zephyr is now happy somewhere in Rainbow Bridge and perhaps her soul has already found love with her guardian in a new body.

My own story with my animals reflects that sometimes they do ask to be helped to pass over.

I used to have an African Pygmy hedgehog called Zoe. She was an adorable companion, full of character and mischief, very aware of her own mind and very determined too. We had five blissful years together. The last few months of her life were the most difficult and yet the most powerful time I ever had with an animal.

On the morning of her passing, thoughts came straight away in my mind: *It is time for me to go, let me go please, I need help to leave this body.* With tears rolling down my cheeks, I made an emergency appointment with the vet, who confirmed our worst fear and I had to say my final goodbyes to my little soulmate.

I since have adopted two Persians rescue cats, and one of them was born the same year as Zoe passed, and some of the things he does reminds me of her. Could it be that she has found her way home again? Perhaps it is wishful thinking, but deep inside I do believe she hasn't left us. She's somewhere around us, and she's definitively in our hearts.

Carol Schultz

www.carolschultz.com

I live in Pekin, Illinois, with my daughter and two cats, Augie and Blinky, and I'm a professional animal communicator. I've done this since 2000, serving clients throughout my home state of Illinois, in other parts of the Midwest and across the US. My desire to assist animals and their human companions is inspired by my feline companion, Panda, a graceful, wise and playful friend, who passed into spirit when my journey on this path began.

When Panda went into sudden kidney failure, I was devastated and emotional. At the time I knew someone who had the capability to communicate the thoughts and feelings of animals. This counsellor let me know Panda's thoughts about what I was doing to assist her and it helped us both through a very difficult six-week period. Near the end of Panda's life, I began to pick up her thoughts myself. It was a total joy for us both to have this connection.

When the time came to help Panda with her physical passing, this heart-to-heart and mind-to-mind connection made the experience one of understanding and discovery, rather than of complete sorrow. It was a wonderful gift. At that point I received the confirmation that this connection with animals and Nature was part of my life purpose, along with helping others to connect with their animal companions in the same way.

Following these profound experiences and realizations, I transitioned into working more closely with animals. I became a veterinary assistant with a local animal rehabilitation clinic, a pet-sitter and also a volunteer at animal sanctuaries.

Early on in my journey as an animal communicator, I began facilitating courses to help others regain their telepathic ability and confidence to communicate with animals. My passion to educate and support others who desire a deeper connection with their own companions has resulted in thousands of students participating in these courses. I'm very honoured to now have numerous professional animal communicators and holistic animal healers as my peers, who began their path as students seeking this both magical and scientific connection with their companions.

My motivation is compassion for all beings and a desire to help all species understand each other better, particularly to help restore the lost human ability to freely and directly communicate with other species.

Remaining open to surprises and profound healings, I have noticed that sometimes the smallest nuances can be the cosmic key that unlocks an area of healing for both the animal and person. Trust turned that key in one of my very first cases.

Duke the cat greeted me telepathically by barking at the beginning of a client phone session. I reconnected telepathically several times, thinking that possibly my next canine client was arriving early to connect, but I kept receiving the same response: barking. I stepped back telepathically and checked in with myself again to ensure I was grounded and neutral, and yet the barking continued. Trusting, I addressed the barking as Duke, the feline. The door of telepathic communication opened, and Duke, a young personality of much enthusiasm and adventure, came through. He'd wanted to be a dog, which explained some of his unfriendly and frustrating behaviour with other cats in the house.

Acknowledging Duke in this way went a long way towards establishing more harmony in the home, as interactions with other cat family members notably improved following the session.

A large part of my practice is related to clients connecting with animals close to passing on.

One of my clients, Margaret, was struggling with the loss of her long-time canine companion, Lady. She shared stories and pictures with me about their life together, and Lady wanted to share her memories as well! Lady assured Margaret that she was doing well and was surrounded by angelic support and nurturing. She described being in a majestic cathedral with gorgeous marble pillars and floors, a place filled with formality and traditions. In conveying this to Margaret, it was clear validation to her that Lady was safe and in a place of spiritual rest. A weight was visibly lifted for them both.

Eventually, Lady returned in a new physical body to enjoy the earthly realm with Margaret once again. There was a period of time before Lady's reincarnation when she indicated that she was coming back as a feline, with an intention to be an easy-to-care-for companion as Margaret enjoyed retirement. However, energies shifted prior to her physical return, and Lady chose to return as a very perky and active puppy. Margaret was thrilled beyond measure to be reconnected with her dear companion, now named Chloe, and have young and lively energy to brighten her life.

Lost animal cases are another area where I serve clients. There are both difficulties and rewards in supporting someone who is searching for a lost companion. Over the years I have developed an approach that works well for me. I have also found that some students really have a strong talent for lost animal cases, which I encourage to blossom.

For lost animal cases, I typically approach the session as a 20- to 30-minute connection. This provides an opportunity to receive first impressions regarding the potential condition and whereabouts of the lost animal and convey energetic guidance on how to assist in reconnecting the client with their companion. This process of working with lost animals continuously evolves.

Lost animal cases tend to be accompanied by strong emotional stress factors, so it's important for the animal to sense their person being grounded and centred during the conversation. This will enhance the communication exchange, and subsequent search.

In one lost animal case, Boise and Clyde, indoor/outdoor cats, set out on an adventure in the middle of a Chicago winter. Each time I spoke to them they reassured me they were fine, warm enough and finding food. They also said they knew the way home and could get there, but after a couple of conversations it became apparent that they were waiting for something to change at home. Their human caretaker Joanne needed to make some changes in her life and, according to Boise and Clyde, their ongoing absence was meant to be the catalyst.

The cats were gone for a chilling three weeks and there was a distinct sign when they were about to return. About 20 to 30 minutes into some serious discussion, I felt a huge shift energetically, and actually heard a pop, like a vacuum sealed jar opening. Conveying this to Joanne, Boise and Clyde communicated that they would now return home, and they concluded the session. I didn't know how long they would be, but lo and behold, the following morning Boise poked into the window left open for his return. He took off again, but shortly thereafter, apparently after Boise gave Clyde the 'all clear', both cats came trotting in together, as if nothing had happened.

My advice to clients and students is to trust your intuition, listen to your heart and spend quiet time with your animals, Nature and yourself. Honour who you are, nurture yourself, let go and have fun.

Animals see your heart, past the things that distract us from our core. Trust the animals as teachers and compassionate reminders of the love and balance that are continuously available when we pause and notice.

Niki Senior

www.animalmagictraining.com

'What on Earth are you doing with that cat?' This was a phrase I would undoubtedly hear almost every day from my parents, from the time when I was aged about eight when my dad bought home a scrawny, black semi-feral cat to 'keep me company'. As an only child with extremely busy parents, I would occupy myself by reading anything on the subject of animals. I'd hide myself away in my bedroom and have my nose in a mountain of non-fiction books.

One day, Dad, who worked as a builder at a city steelworks, had taken over the task of feeding the foundry cats from his colleague, who'd gone on holiday. All of them were stray cats who had been carelessly cast aside into this harsh, industrial landscape, from homes that perhaps they'd thought would be theirs forever.

A black cat that I later named Timmy had a big impact on my dad. Timmy was semi-feral, and although my dad tried to coax him to eat, his appetite was poor. After hiring a trapping cage, Dad rescued Timmy and brought him home. I was overjoyed to have a companion to share silly moments and secrets with. We bonded almost straight away, but after a week we had to take Timmy to see the vet because he was losing weight drastically and his appetite was increasingly poor. After numerous tests over a few days, Timmy was diagnosed with a renal tumour. He was given an injection and a few pills, and we were advised that we should expect Timmy to live no more than three or four months. We were also told that the life Timmy had suffered had most likely contributed to his condition. The vet asked to see Timmy again in another four weeks and indicated that we should decide what we wanted to do. We took Timmy home. I was devastated. How could I allow this little man to suffer? What could I possibly do to help him? I couldn't just leave him to die, could I? Unaware of what I was doing, I placed Timmy in his basket and sat at the side of him, placed my hands upon him and immediately felt immense, almost pulsating energy flow through me. Timmy started to 'heat up and buzz'. It was akin to a light being turned on. Mum looked at me and obviously thought it was such a strange thing to do, but to me it was natural. I held out my hands, lightly touching Timmy's tiny body for around 10 minutes, until I saw his expression turn almost serene, and then I stroked him from head to tail.

Each day after school I'd rush in and demonstrate what I now know is healing with Timmy. After about a week Timmy started to pick up, raise his head in interest at food and start to eat, and he even began to play with pieces of string that I'd pull across the floor for him. In fact, he started to behave like a normal, healthy feline! Four weeks passed and upon our visit to the vet, as he prodded and poked my little friend, the vet had quite a perplexed look upon his face. 'I'd like to run a couple more tests,' he said. With the result of the tests, a rather bemused vet told us that the previously satsuma-sized renal tumour was now the size of a pea. How could this be? The vet said he hadn't seen anything like it, and he couldn't offer us an explanation. Was it the injection at the initial consultation? Was it the two weeks' worth of painkillers? Was it the energy that I had channelled? I honestly can't say, and neither could the vet at that time. One thing I do know is that Timmy went on to live another eight years and finally passed to Rainbow Bridge peacefully in his sleep, aged 16!

Prior to us having Timmy, when I was about three or four I remember Mum telling me that on our way to nursery school she'd be shooing away the cats that would jump off gate posts to follow me. I also remember a time when Mum was late to collect me from school when I was about nine and I was waiting at the school gates when all the other children had gone home. Sitting beside me was a Dalmatian, which I later found out was named Jason, and a border collie, called Dilly. It was as if the dogs knew Mum would be late and wanted to keep me safe. I was also always the one in my circle of friends to ask to take the neighbours' dogs for a walk rather than to play with dolls.

Upon leaving school I went straight to college to study business and finance, and then went to work within the Social Services. I gained little from my post, and the stress it created led me to have a mild stroke aged just 24. I refused all medication and sought holistic methods of healing and recuperation. I also looked within myself. I did self-healing every day, meditation and visualization, and I also had regular reflexology and Reiki healing treatments. When I'd healed my body and felt stronger within myself, I decided that the stroke was a turning-point in my life and I embarked upon a change of career. I trained for the next eight years in various modalities of complementary therapy and in psychological counselling, and I also trained for two years in Reiki healing and became a Reiki Master Teacher. That was 14 years ago.

Throughout my twenties I found my diary divided between animal clients and human ones. I worked with a varying range of species from horses, dogs, cats and other domestic animals to llamas, alpacas, snakes and marmoset monkeys, travelling throughout the UK to see animals and their human companions.

Meditation helped me tremendously with my recovery to good health, and during it I received great inspirational messages and guidance, telling me that I had to pass on knowledge to others to define and validate the work that I was doing. I needed to express a language of what I was doing from the heart and help others tap into this great energy within themselves. In 1998 I received what can only be called 'an awakening', and I knew that this was the path on which I had to walk.

I knew in my heart that many people wanted to share this deeper bond with their own animals and indeed the whole of the animal kingdom, and to recognize that they were not separate from these creatures. So for three years I worked devising a professional animal-healing training course.

I believe that anyone can achieve great things in animal healing. You need not possess a 'gift'; we all have the gift if we just tap into a part of ourselves that has lain dormant for so long. Healing is a re-awakening of mind. It is learning to trust our own spirit and intuition. It is also believing that great things are possible. I have seen some near-miracles since I first helped heal Timmy 30 years ago.

A quiet and relaxed mind must be the basis of a deeper connection to our animal companions. Furthermore, any notion that animals are lesser beings must be swept aside. Animals should be nurtured and cared for if we are to share our lives with them.

Animals are no way beneath us. They should not be persecuted in any way or used for monetary gain, or indeed suffer untimely death or be slaughtered for human consumption. If you want to develop a deeper bond, then please think a while on the previous sentence, as it deserves great thought and compassion. Having an animal show unconditional love for us can have a deep effect on our personalities. Cats don't care how we look or if we have put on an extra few pounds and dogs don't care how untidy the kitchen drawers are. Their connection with us is deep and will be everlasting. We can tap into this unconditional love and energy simply by placing our hands upon them, sensing their energy and becoming a part of it.

I'm truly blessed to be learning and teaching something which, I believe, I was put on this Earth for – to work as a full-time animal healer. Upon my journey I have met with personal struggles, but the blessings far outweigh any adversity. I've met some wonderful souls, both animal and human, who've played a major part in my past, present and also my future life. These thanks go to them. I am forever indebted to that scrawny black semi-feral cat named Timmy, but for whom I wouldn't be living my dream now. Thank you, Timmy, you taught me so much, you shared your heart and soul with me, you are forever my guide.

The stories above are from professional animal communicators, but some people, like those below, have a natural ability that they just use on a personal and gentle level.

Tracey's story

I've always loved animals from as soon as I could walk. I never had any pets of my own until I was at primary school, but my grandparents had dogs and cats. My mum said when I was a baby she would take me round to see my grandparents and put me down to sleep in their bedroom. If I cried my granddad's boxer dog, Caesar, would start barking at my mum until she'd go and make sure that I was all right. Caesar and Sandy, the golden Labrador, always looked after me as I grew up. They were so gentle and I loved them to bits.

My mum said I was always stroking dogs and cats when I was little, and she was sometime scared as she would turn around and I'd be petting some big dog. My mum said I was lucky I never got bitten. I was never scared of animals and I think I never got bitten because I loved them all and they knew it. I can remember when I was about three or four and we went to Knole Park, and I went up to the deer, including a big stag, and stroked them. I have a picture of me and the stag.

Tracey reminds me of myself. I had this kind of empathy from a very young age. I think a lot of people do, but aren't encouraged, and so their talents and connections get rusty, which is a shame.

Peggy's story

My mom was warned not to let a cat sleep with a child, as they were said to climb on their faces, but she didn't have much choice with Simba, our lion-like Burmese cat. These cats are very vocal and if Mom tried to put me to bed without Simba, the yowling (from the cat!) could be heard all down the street. So, she gave in, but watched us closely. There was never a problem, although I always tell people don't do this with your kid! Just in case!

I was two before I really realized that I had a cat as a bedtime companion, and of course I thought it was perfectly normal. It wasn't until I got to three and became a chatterbox that things got really weird. In the mornings I would tell my mom things like she was going to drop a cereal bowl and would blame Simba for it. Of course, she then tripped over Simba at breakfast and she did blame him. Soon Mom asked me how I knew the little things that were going to happen. I think it freaked her out. I don't know if she was more freaked out or less when I replied that Simba had told me! I will never forget that cat.

I sometimes think that if all the people who had this natural talent developed it more, and used it more widely, the animal kingdom might become very much better off!

Chapter 7

Dogs and Cats That Return from Spirit

I often have people write and tell me about their sick pets, and how they can't bear to let the animal go. Or they write to tell me they did make this very tough decision and are now wracked with guilt as to whether they did the right thing.

I went through the same thing with my doggy soulmate, Ace. I kept putting off having her put to sleep because I couldn't bear the thought of being without her, of being 'responsible' for her death or of letting her go perhaps prematurely and living with the guilt of that. I worried that because she still sometimes seemed to be enjoying herself I should let her continue. It was my son, Phillip, who put things into perspective for me when he said, 'Just because she's able to smile now and then, it doesn't mean her life is worth living the rest of the time.' In the wild, sick, old or injured animals are quickly dispatched by Nature. Having taken animals out of the wild and tamed them through domestication, we owe it to them to take the place of Nature. So, when the time is right and they no longer enjoy life, we have to stop their suffering.

Our pets seem to know when we can't possibly let go of them after they have died. They come back from the other side to show us that they and other souls we miss, still love us, and to bring us comfort when we need it by staying around until we're ready to move on or they can guide us onto a new path. This is one of the things that proves to me that they do have souls.

Some pets we're very close to also contain a part of our soul, and as such we cannot be severed from them. They will always be there next to us. It doesn't mean they're not happy or not moving on either, because all of us, whether we're living here at the time or not, keep a part of ourselves in spirit. That part can always be in touch and it wouldn't matter if your pets had moved into new bodies – a part of them could still connect with you. They're sending the messages because they love you and have found a way to talk to you.

Emma's story

I went to Oxford Castle with a paranormal group a week after I had lost my beloved golden retriever, Shadow, who was my best friend. He looked exactly like the dog on the front of your first pet book, *Pets Have Souls Too*, so I knew that it must be fate that I read the book when I saw it!

Shadow died suddenly. He went in for a routine op and the vet found lots of inoperable tumours, so with a heavy heart my family had to make the decision to let him go. I wasn't there at the time, as I was working in a shop. I was on my own and a spirit came to me, and I suddenly knew it was Shadow, but I wouldn't believe it. I said aloud, 'Whoever is there, just cross over, OK?' Then at the end of my shift I went home and my mum told me my Shadow had died.

A week later I was at Oxford Castle again and we were using a Ouija board. Shadow came through, he came to me. That morning I'd walked past his picture and had said to him, 'Don't you dare come through. You stay over there!' Nevertheless, the planchette went to the S, then back to the middle, then to the H and it spelled out his name. I said, 'Oh my God! It's him, he's here.' No one believed me. They thought I was mad. They wouldn't even comfort me, but just looked at me as if I was insane. I was hysterical, trying to ask my dog questions, but I couldn't stop crying. I asked him if he was on the other side and he replied that he was. I asked him if Granny was with him and he said yes. I then told him, 'It's OK, you can go now' and, just as obedient as he'd always been in life, he went.

Later on a member of the group asked me, 'How could a dog come through?' She didn't believe me. I imagine she didn't believe that dogs survived death. All I could think of to say to her, in my distress, was that in life he was really intelligent.

Losing an animal you're so close to is very traumatic. I think it's very sweet that Shadow tried so hard to comfort his mistress.

Joanie's story

We had a small Yorkie – Yorkshire Terrier – called Pippin, whom we had for 15 happy years, and then because of ill-health we decided it was better for her sake to have her put to sleep. She was taken to the vet's the next morning and quietly and gently put into her last sleep. That evening my husband and I were sitting watching television, when out of the corner of my eye I spotted Pippin's little Yorkie tail disappearing into the bedroom, just as it always had at her usual time of 9 p.m. I remarked to my husband that I thought I had seen Pippin going off to bed, and he answered me with a smile on his face, telling me he'd noticed her too, disappearing round the corner of his chair beside the fire.

Several years before that my step-daughter, Amanda, had passed away. She was only 28 years old when she died, and was always close to Pippin. A few days after Amanda died we were interested to see that Pippin kept looking towards the other end of our sitting room as if she could see someone there. She kept walking up and down as if looking up at someone and we felt that there was someone other than us in the room.

We also had a big black fluffy cat called Fudge, at the same time as we had Pippin. The two animals were very close, to the point that they would curl up with each other on the settee. Fudge was put to sleep at the grand old age of 17 years old. Like most cats, Fudge loved to catch birds, which always upset us so we bought a small bell to slot on his collar to warn the birds away when he was approaching. The evening of the day he was put to sleep we heard his bell tinkling around the kitchen where he usually slept, and again during the night after we retired to bed. This lasted for a few days, then stopped.

My hubby passed away four years ago and even now when I receive messages from him, it's always mentioned that there's a small Yorkshire Terrier by his side.

It's very comforting to know that we'll all be reunited with our very special pets as well as our loved ones after we pass over.

Melanie's story

My daughter was due to be born the same day we had our black-and-white cat, Pixie, put to sleep. It was a bitter-sweet time. Pixie had been our surrogate child all the time we never thought we could have one of our own. Her fur was often wet with my tears when another IVF hadn't worked. But finally the miracle happened, and our baby girl was born.

We fought an urge to call our little girl Pixie, and named her Jessica instead. We never mentioned Pixie to Jessica, but when Jessica was 15 years old she said she wanted to ask me a question. It sounded serious so I was expecting it to be about boys. But it wasn't. Jessica wanted to know if we had ever had a black-and-white cat, so I told her that we had, before she was born. 'Oh,' she said, seeming puzzled. 'That's odd because I could have sworn you had one after I was born and I've often felt the urge to ask about it. When I was about two or three I went through a period of having night frights, and every time it happened, this black-and-white cat would come into the room and sit with me until I went to sleep.'

Of course, I was staggered and so happy to think my Pixie hadn't gone for good after all but had stayed around to look after our child.

That gave me goosebumps! I feel so humbled by animals sometimes, their generosity of spirit puts a lot of humans to shame. Pixie still cared for Melanie and her new baby years after she had passed.

Lynda's story

Let me tell you what happened to my family some 11 years ago. My sister's husband died from a brain aneurysm. He was only in his early fifties and his children were still at school. It was a traumatic time for everyone, especially for my sister, and my mum, who loved him like a son. We all felt his passing, but we didn't realize how much the family dog, a mini foxie (Fox Terrier) named Bogart, was affected by his loss.

When Greg was alive he used to take Bogart for long, wonderful walks and sometimes, when it was a hot day, would even smuggle him into the local pub when he went for a refreshing pint. After

Greg's death, Bogart would climb up on my sister's chest and comfort her with his presence.

Sometime after the funeral, the family decided to go to the cemetery to pay Greg a visit. Bogart came along. The cemetery is spread over a vast area, and we searched for the tree that was our marker. Finding the tree was no problem, but we all agreed that we had no idea exactly where Greg was buried. It was just row upon row upon row of plots. We opened the car door and out shot Bogart. He's only little, so he quickly disappeared from our sight. We decided to search for Bogart before restarting our search for Greg's grave. Then we heard it – a terrible and distressed howling that was coming from one of the rows. We followed the noise and, to our astonishment and shock, found little Bogart on Greg's plot, all four paws planted firmly, head raised high and howling over and over again. At the time we were all very frightened and distressed by what we saw. There was Greg's little mate, who'd not only found his grave from among the thousands of plots but was crying out to him at the top of his voice. How did he find Greg, who was buried in a family plot with the concrete on his grave well and truly set?

My sister never took Bogart back to the cemetery. Bogart's coming up to 12 – do you think we should take him again to see his dad?

This beautiful story made me cry and I replied to Lynda that it seemed to me Bogart felt he had never had the chance to say goodbye to Greg and so he took the opportunity to do so in his own way – by howling. Perhaps his 'dad's' spirit was hanging around the grave, waiting for the time when Lynda would bring his boy there and Bogart sensed this. I thought it was most likely that if she took him there again he would be much calmer because he had already said goodbye. I also felt Bogart's connection to Greg would strengthen as he aged, and assured Lynda that when it was time for Bogart to go, Greg would be waiting for him with open arms.

Lil' Aug's story

When I was a little girl I would draw pictures of a German shepherd, a wolf-like dog with bright eyes and perky ears. I didn't know why I was drawing these pictures, but I just felt a need to. I told everyone that this was going to be my future dog one day.

Years later, my mother and father brought a puppy home with them. As soon as I saw this little wolf-like pup, my eyes lit up in excitement. I felt an instant attachment to this puppy, as though I'd known her before. We called her Mandy.

As Mandy grew up, she resembled the drawings I used to make as a little girl. She even had the same bright eyes, so much so that my mother used to nickname her Bright Eyes. Mandy was a very intelligent dog. We really do think she had some wolf breeding in her. A woman we met in Canada who raised wolves mentioned that to us once. She said Mandy's mannerisms were just like the wolf pups'.

Sometime later, we had to put Mandy to sleep. Too many over-the-counter snacks we had given her had brought on diabetes. We didn't know she had it, but eventually she wasn't even able to walk any longer. While I was at work that dark day, I felt Mandy's presence with me outside my workplace. I thought how odd that was, as she wasn't supposed to be euthanized until later that afternoon. I still felt her presence with me, sitting with me on the sidewalk during my lunch break at 12:30 p.m., so I called my mother, who confirmed that they'd decided to put Mandy to sleep early, at midday. I cried my eyes out in grief.

Months later, around 2 a.m. one January night, I was awakened from my sleep by some strong energy in our home. While lying in bed with my eyes open, I heard Mandy's familiar wolf-like howl downstairs in our living room. I didn't know at the time that my mother (who sleeps downstairs) had also heard her. I sent out a thought to Mandy and called out to her in my mind. I said, 'Mandy, if that is you, come upstairs and be with me!' Suddenly I felt a rush of energy near the left side of my bed. I felt this feeling of excitement, and relief and joy. And I felt her lick my face, not exactly a physical sensation, but still an energy-like feeling that a dog was licking my face. I sensed her emotion. I eventually fell back asleep with a smile on my face, but never shared this experience with anyone in my family, including my mother, until some time had passed.

It was only because some weeks later my mother suddenly blurted out in the car that she'd heard Mandy howl in the living room weeks previously. I stared at her with my mouth open while my father joked that she was losing it mentally. Then I interrupted and told her how I'd heard Mandy, too. We both looked at each other and realized from that day forward that animals have souls, and that they live on as humans do.

Mandy was my soul sister. Whether in another life, or in the heavenly realms of the Great Spirit, I know that we knew each other before, and we'll see each other again.

It's funny how sometimes animals will work to bring evidence not only to people who are open to believing, but also to others who aren't. The timing of her 'appearances' by Mandy appears to be a deliberate way to do this.

Shelley's story

I've loved and lost many pets through the years, but one incident that sticks out most in my mind is about a little Cocker Spaniel named Crystal, who belonged to my then husband. He'd had Crystal since childhood and, shortly after we were married, my husband's parents decided to bring her from Kansas to Texas to live with us. The trouble was, by then Crystal was very old, sick and blind, and when she arrived at our house she had no idea where she was or who we were. By that time she was thin, shaking and completely incontinent and, unfortunately, because of the mess she would make we had to keep her outside much of the time, which literally broke my heart. I remember many nights sitting at the kitchen table crying over that poor little dog. We absolutely did not know what to do for her.

A couple of months passed and it became apparent that Crystal was getting worse and seemed to be in pain. She limped on all her legs and, although she never complained, it was obviously getting unbearable. I took her to the vet who, of course, suggested we put her to sleep. I'd never had to do anything like that before. My pets had normally either died of natural causes or had got lost over the years, and I was not sure what to think about such drastic measures. I came home and told my husband about it and we cried some more, wondering all the while what would be the best course of action. I spent a long time thinking about this issue, and whether or not it's OK to assist our furry friends in their transition. I know this is a controversial subject for some and that there are many opinions about the topic.

After thinking it over, I've come to feel we take better care of our pets at times than we do of each other. There is a time to live and a time to die, and unfortunately, since our animals are innocents, there is no real way for them to communicate with us to let us know what they need, how they feel and what they would want to have happen at the end of their lives. Personally, I feel some of the treatments we give our animals to sustain their lives are inhumane because they have no way to understand what is being done to them or why. They only know they are away from us – the ones they love – and being tortured and hurt by needles, tubes and treatments, which eventually will not avoid the inevitable.

My mom and I took Crystal to the vet late one morning and sat with her as the vet administered the shot. Her breathing slowed down and I could see her pain was gone. Right at the end, she opened her eyes, looked up at me and seemed to say, 'Thank you.' It's a blink in time I will never forget. It was a good death, a peaceful transition.

Within moments she was gone, and that's when the miracle happened: I suddenly heard a whooshing sound as her soul departed from her body. At first I couldn't believe it, but then the room was filled with peace, and I felt glad she was finally at rest and could run and play in the grassy fields of Heaven. At that moment, any doubt as to whether or not I'd done the right thing melted away. She was at peace, out of pain and no longer suffering. It's tough to say goodbye, harder to let go, but in the end it brought peace to both of us.

I've spent time working as a hospice volunteer and experienced many unusual and mystical experiences in my life, but of all of the things I've seen, I think this experience with Crystal was one of the most important. It showed me that we really are unlimited souls who survive bodily death, and that these forms we take while here in the physical plane are not who we truly are. We are infinite, and so are our furry friends. We will all meet again one day in the energetic life of the hereafter, and what a gloriously happy day that will be!

Shelley's story reminds us of the duty of care we all have to our pets and also demonstrates that a pet's passing can bring us great comfort through the spiritual insights it can reveal.

Lisa's story

Our beloved cat, Tara, was a bit of a wanderer, and one evening he was knocked down and killed instantly. We were very distraught and buried him in our front garden. His brother is still alive to this day. We decided straight away to get another cat, and went to the shelter, as we always do, believing that it's better to home an unwanted animal than to pay for a pedigree and encourage their breeding. We went into the cattery that day, and there among an array of young cats we saw this black beauty who pushed her way to the front, her eyes looking as though she knew us. In effect, she picked us! From day one she developed her own personality and the characteristics that made 'Panther' the extremely special cat she was.

She developed a taste for cheese-and-onion crisps, which she would even gently take from my mouth. She also had a taste for Chinese food! One day for a joke we asked if she wanted either cat food or curry. Her eyes lit up at the mention of curry! At meal times she would come running as soon as she heard the knocking sound I made with my knife. She waited patiently for her treat. Mealtimes thus became very funny, as if she knew in advance what was coming.

She always curled up on the quilt next to me when I was in bed, and seemed to talk to me with her eyes. Like most cats she would quite often sleep for long periods. She loved to roll over and let me stroke her belly, often chirping at me. She also enjoyed playing with leaves in the wind on the lawn, but all the time she would keep checking to see where I was. She sometimes accompanied me into the bathroom, where she'd lie behind my head and enjoy my taste of music, such as Status Quo, as I soaked in the hot water. She even seemed to dance with me. In effect, we became inseparable.

Sadly, she was taken from us in March 2009 at the age of 13, following a short illness. She died in my bedroom, with me holding her paw, and even now I well up at the thought of that time. However, I feel she's never really left me. I get a breeze from where she lay on my bed, which is stronger when she answers me. She lets me know she's still with me all the time. When we go out for coffee her head appears to be etched in the foam in the cup as if to say, 'I'm here with you.' The impression of her shape regularly appears on the cushion and quilt as if she's still present. She's around me constantly and playing with me. I find her messages a comfort and remain fiercely loyal to her memory.

It is lovely that Lisa gets so much comfort from a cat that's no longer with her except in spirit.

Hayley's story

In October 1987 a farrier friend of mine took me to work with him one day. On the farm where he was working there was a litter of six-week-old German Shepherd puppies. The owner told me, 'Don't go near the runt, there's something wrong with her. She was born 14 hours after the rest of the litter and she's aggressive.'

Well, I couldn't believe a six-week-old pup could possibly be aggressive, but when we approached her she snapped and snarled like a wild thing. I sat down and played with the pups, and the next thing the 'aggressive runt' was sitting on my lap! They couldn't believe it when I played with her and she was so sweet. I got a phone call two weeks later and the owner asked me if I wanted her as she was going to be euthanized because no one could approach her. Obviously, I said yes immediately. I really needed someone to put my love into my life as it was so empty without Storm, my much-missed pony that had died of liver failure. They had already named her, because of her temperament, and when I asked what, they told me her name was Stormi.

She was a very old soul and never had to be taught anything. She was a perfect lady and loved everyone. When she was just 14 weeks old, I got up in the morning and went to wake her and found that she'd died in the night. The post-mortem revealed massive liver failure.

Move on to 2009... I went for a walk with a group of Rhodesian Ridgeback owners in a park. In comes a lady I'd never met before, whose name was Cheryl, and with her were three puppies. I was not in the market for another dog! Whenever Cheryl called them she said 'Woza!' a Zulu word meaning 'come here,' and this was just one of her many eccentricities! Anyway, at the end of the walk she approached me and asked if I'd be interested in the pup that had black mask-like markings. I was very restrained and didn't snatch him and run!

We went home and discussed it and then went to collect him the following day. The entire time we sat in the kitchen having coffee and discussing the terms of ownership, the puppy sat framed in the window on a bed, watching. He was going to be called Zorro, due to the mask, which means fox (my surname) in Spanish. Cheryl's husband called him 'Bakkies', an Afrikaans word that means face or mask, due to his black face, or 'Mombakkies', which is literally 'mask' or, rudely, 'face ache'! Anyway, Bakkies he became, because Zorro just didn't suit him.

Again, this was a dog that I had to teach nothing. He was a very serious, very, very old soul and my constant companion. When I fed the horses and donkeys, he'd carry the bucket of food for me. He was a dog everyone loved.

There's an autistic girl, Lauren, who is about 20, whose mom does dog-training with me. Lauren would sit and watch the class. Bakkies would go sit next to her with his head in her lap. The first time she ever spoke in front of people other than her family was to him, and then to me, to ask about him. He was just that sort of dog. Whenever we went for a walk he'd seek out empty cans of lager and drink the dregs. He had a real taste for lager! He was six months old when I came home one day to find that he stank like the cellar in a pub. He'd found two crates of beer in my laundry room on top of the freezer, knocked them down and, between him and two others, had opened and drunk almost the whole contents of 32 cans! When the vet finished laughing he assured me the dogs would be fine, but would have a horrible hangover the following day.

The following day Bakkies was really not well. I had to go to dog-training that evening and thought I'd leave him at home as he was ill. However, he really wanted to come, so off we went. On my way home, at nearly 8 p.m. in the pitch dark, I had to stop at a very slow-moving traffic light. The dogs were lying down fast asleep in the back. Next thing I knew, a hand came through my window, grabbed me by the throat and was going for my car keys. There was another man on the other side trying to get the passenger door open, too. Now, the best result would have been for just my car to have been taken but, unfortunately, it seemed more likely that I was going to be abducted and suffer all that went with that.

The next thing I knew, something came over the back of my seat and attacked the man who had his hand around my throat – it was the most terrifying sight I've ever seen in my life. Six-month-old Bakkies attacked him so viciously that there was blood all over the car. Luckily, both men then ran off into the night and somehow I managed to drive home.

I had just two weeks of bragging rights – and you better believe I boasted about having my life saved by this baby. Then, one day, I was outside with him and he suddenly screamed and fell down, screeching all the while. Within 30 seconds my Bakkies was dead. The post-mortem showed he had died from an extremely rare non-congenital heart defect. The vets were amazed and had to consult specialists around the world to put a name to it.

The night after he died, once I eventually got to sleep, I had a dream. Bakkies came from behind one of my outbuildings with the tiniest, funniest-looking, weirdest-coloured little Ridgeback bitch puppy (I'm not a fan of bitches) with a red ribbon round her neck. He 'told' me her name was 'Mouse', and if I didn't believe him I was to 'ask Scout' (my African grey parrot). Then he walked away and left this little scrap sitting in front of me, staring up at me. I woke up and I was devastated. I got up and went through to the living room. As my daughter and I walked in my parrot looked at me and said 'Woza', (the word Cheryl used to call her pups) as clear as a bell, even though he'd never heard that word in his life.

Not long afterwards I got a call from Cheryl, inviting me to go look at a litter of one of her bitch's pups. They all had homes lined up, but she wanted me to just come and see them. We went outside and there was the little scrap with a red ribbon, just like in my dream. It took all my power not to burst into tears, as I knew they all had homes, but there was 'Mouse' clear as day. I honestly thought my heart was going to break. The entire time we sat inside she sat framed in the window looking in, exactly as Bakkies had done before her. I didn't say anything as I didn't want Cheryl to feel she had to either give me the pup or disappoint me because she was already spoken for.

When I got into the car, much to my husband's distress, I burst into tears. I told him, 'I've just seen Mouse, but she's got a home!' He replied, 'Listen, I don't know which one she was, but Cheryl asked me if you'd be interested in the little girl with the red ribbon.' Apparently, she'd asked him to broach the subject with me as she didn't want me to take a pup if it wasn't the right one! I jumped at the chance and now I have 'Mhousse' (spelled this way for numerology reasons).

I know Bakkies is still around. Scout regularly says 'Woza', but only when I'm feeling a bit low or sad. A while after Bakkies died, the light above 'his' chair started to come on and go off randomly. My husband is an electrician and has checked it, to curb my still-present doubts, but there's no fault in it. If I take photos of other dogs sleeping on 'Bakkies' chair', there is always an orb there or thereabouts. I'd never taken a photo with an orb in it before, so when I got the first one, two weeks before he died, I thought something was wrong with the camera.

This story from South Africa made me both cry and smile. It's very sad that Hayley seemed to have lost so many much-loved pets, but they all seem to have come to her for a purpose. I feel that the original Storm came back in several other bodies in order to be there at that moment, in that situation, with Hayley, to save her as Bakkies did. Hopefully, she'll have a long and trouble-free association with Mhousse now that incident has passed.

Stephanie's story

We adopted Lucy, a four-year-old Cocker Spaniel that was looking for a new home after her owners split. Tony, my husband, and I took her into our home and our hearts and for almost five years we lived as one. We had both retired a year prior to Lucy arriving, and had all the time in the world to help her settle into her new home – which was quite a task, such was her loyalty to her first owners.

We adored her, and she adored us. She was never more than a few feet away from me at any one time. Then suddenly, one June day, she developed breathing problems, which turned out to be the symptoms of serious heart failure, and she was not expected to live through the night. However, miraculously she made it and, with medication, her life returned to normal within a few short days.

All seemed well, but then something strange occurred on 10 December, when my husband was out and Lucy was reposing on a cream velvet armchair. We had a glass door and a glass window in the lounge, which looked into the hall. Suddenly, Lucy stood up on the chair and wagged her tail in absolute joy. I saw that she was looking out of the door and whatever she was looking at must have moved, as she then shifted her gaze to the window. Certain that my husband must have returned home, I left the room to greet him, only to find that there was no one there. I was seriously spooked by this and, when he eventually did return, I told him I feared Lucy was going to die because it seemed that someone had come for her. That was on the Wednesday and, sure enough, on the Saturday she died. We're convinced some person or animal came for her and whoever it was brought her utter joy, which is some comfort.

After we'd buried her in the garden, my husband was making good the ground, re-laying the turf as I watched anxiously from the house and to my amazement I could see that he was smiling. When he came in he said that the strangest thing had happened. Lucy had really liked a special song that he often sang to her, and she would join in by howling, which made us laugh. She loved this, and would sometimes initiate the song by making strange sounds and looking at us expectantly, which was a signal for the song to begin. He said that as he was tending the grave, this song came to him clearly, hence his smile.

During that day, I spoke of my envy that she'd made contact with him. We went to bed to spend the first dreadful night without our girl and as I fell asleep I dreamed, but it was more than a dream. I was back in the lounge with Lucy on the aforementioned chair and although the room was dark, where she was lying there was a bright light. She was licking and fussing me in joyful reunion, but I knew it was not for ever and that she would soon go again. Suddenly we were by the fireplace, which opened up into a dark tunnel, and she disappeared into it. A clock on the mantelpiece tilted forward and a door at the front of it swung open at this moment.

I awoke with a start; my heart was pounding and I was crying. I woke Tony to tell him I'd seen Lucy. He said that in his prayers moments before I had the dream he'd spoken to Lucy, asking her to visit me as I really needed her to. It settled me enormously and made me feel so happy – for a short time. In discussion, we decided that the tilting of the clock and the opening of the door was meant to signify it was time to go, or that her time had come.

During the course of the next week we made enquiries to find another puppy. I was in contact with a breeder who told me she had only one left. I was concerned in case it was the runt of the litter, but she said no, the pup just did not run forward to prospective buyers, but that she certainly was not weak or timid.

All the other puppies mobbed the visitors, but for some reason she just sat back and watched.

We duly went for a viewing and I looked expectantly for a puppy in the background, but could see none. I asked the owner which was the available puppy and, surprised, she laughingly said that it was the one Tony was holding. She had run straight to him! Again, we believe that Lucy had contacted the puppy and told her to hold back until we came. Of course, we bought her.

Nothing more happened, other than the song I mentioned previously came to both of our minds on a quite regular basis that first year, and we knew Lucy was making contact. And on one occasion, when Tony got up to use the bathroom during the night, he glanced across the dark hall into the lounge (we live in a bungalow) and saw Lucy sitting on the back of her chair as she always had done. We accepted that she was visiting us.

As Lucy had died, Tony had picked up a curl of her fur at the vet's. I'd wrapped it up in tissue, folded it over and over again until it was about two inches square, put it into a little suede jewellery bag, tied it tightly and put it under my pillow, where it had remained for a year. On the first anniversary of Lucy's death I decided I would look at the fur again, just to feel the softness once more. I untied the bag and carefully unfolded the tissue, which was almost impossible as I had been lying on it for a year, but I managed to do it and, to my utter shock, there was nothing there, no trace of any fur ever having been there: nothing, zilch. I stared open-mouthed and the only explanation we could think of was that Lucy had taken it, as a way of making contact on that day. When we went to bed that night, Tony asked me if Molly (our new dog) was with me, because he'd just seen a dog at the end of the lounge out of the corner of his eye, but Molly had been with me all the time, so it was clearly another visit from Lucy.

During that night in bed, I woke up and was mulling over the issue of the fur in the little pouch bag, wondering if there could be any other, although I knew in my heart that Lucy had taken it – but you know you try not to fool yourself, you want to be sure. As I thought, I reached under the pillow for the now empty pouch and withdrew my hand quickly as it felt so hot. If I could describe the intensity of the heat I'd say that, had I looked at it, I would have expected it to be glowing, that was the strength of the heat emanating from it. It served to confirm to us that Lucy truly had removed the fur as a way of making contact, and that her energy was still with the bag it had been in for some hours afterwards.

Over the next few days I tried to re-create the incident, reaching under my pillow and making sure that the bag was under my head, but on each occasion the bag was always cold. Since that time, there has been nothing else. It would seem that Lucy saw us through that first awful year, got us happily loving our new Molly and then moved on.

I find it very touching how Lucy wanted to make sure that her owners would find another dog to love after she had died – and wouldn't leave until they did.

Brenda's story

My pet dog, Tinker, was really special to me. He slept on my bed every night and 'guarded' me from even my parents if they popped in to check on me. We lived in the country about half a mile from the main road and the local bus stop. My mum used to take the dogs (we had two) at night to meet my older sister from the last bus. Tinker had a habit of 'slipping his collar'. He was used to roaming free at home and hated having to wear one.

On this particular evening, Mum was going to meet my sister from the bus and I had an awful premonition that Tinker would die if he went with her. I pleaded with her not to take him and to only take our other dog, but she insisted, telling me not to be so silly. I just knew I wouldn't see him again. That night, as my sister got off the bus across the road, Tinker got very excited to see her and slipped his collar, then ran across the road to greet her, right in front of a tanker. My premonition came true.

I still sense he's with me sometimes at night when I'm in bed. It feels like I can't push my feet down in the bed because he's sitting on it, and I just know it is him. I lost Tinker when I was only about 14, but I remember that night as if it were yesterday. But I take comfort in knowing that Tinker never has to wear a collar now.

How tragic that such a close partnership came to such an early end. However, Brenda has ended up having her dog with her for much longer than his lifetime. I know that in years to come he will still be waiting for her to join him and will be there meet her when she does.

CHAPTER 8

Dogs and Cats That Are Telepathic

Did you ever have a dog or cat that seemed to know what you were thinking? That seemed to either mirror how you were feeling, or went out of its way to change how you were feeling with its own personality and energy? If you listen to the world's best trainer, who in my opinion is Caesar Milan, he will say that energy travels, that training your pet is really just a matter of transposing your energy onto it. In other words, if you are calm, your pet will be, too, and if you are excitable and unbalanced they will be, too. I think he's right, but I would go even further.

There are many proven case of cats and dogs that know, for instance, when their owner is coming home. This isn't because they hear a car and recognize it, as you will see, and not through transference of energy, as the distance is too great for both. The answer has to be telepathy.

You can test your connection to your pet with this, by just waiting until they are settled down somewhere, and then going into another room, and just thinking, 'bring me your toy duck, or pig', or whatever their toy is (see page 42). Make sure you project a picture of that toy in your mind, and then ask and just wait. It might take a while, but you will improve with practice. This can be a very useful tool when you get really good at it. Just imagine if your dog or cat goes missing – that ultimate nightmare of all who love their pets.

How good would it be to ask them to send you a picture in their mind of how and where they are? I have seen this work many times, so it's well worth the effort of establishing a telepathic link. It can be so rewarding to find an ill or injured cat (as they often hide away), or find a dog that had wandered into danger, as if by magic. It isn't magic but it certainly feels like it!

James's story

My dog Moxy is a funny-looking little thing. She resembles a fox but has patchy-coloured fur. She's a bit of a scruff, to be honest, but so cute. Whenever I was on my way home from school, my mom said Moxy would always know I was coming, because she'd jump up at the window and whine. I always thought that meant Moxy was telepathic, but someone told me she could probably just hear the sound of my bike as I turned the last few corners before I got there, which was a bit disappointing.

However, when I was 18 I left home and went away to university, leaving Moxy for the first time. I left Mom, too, and she claimed to be more upset than Moxy was. I missed them both but I was only about 50 miles from home, although it's true I rarely made it there what with the high price of petrol. So Mom worried a lot.

She said it was tough, because when I was home she always knew where I was, if I was safe, if I'd eaten, if I had clean underpants on (!), but with me at university it was like I was nothing to do with her, and she never knew if I was looking after myself, or where I was, or if I got home safe or not.

At first Moxy missed me badly, Mom said, and would pace around at the time I used to get home from school, jumping up and down at the window and fretting for ages, and never really settling for the night. But then, after one afternoon when she'd sat very still for a long time, apparently deep in contemplation, Moxy's behaviour changed. She'd still, at some point every afternoon or evening, react as if I were coming home, but after the usual display she'd just get down from the window and go and lie down quietly, sighing in contentment and quite relaxed. At first Mom thought Moxy was just confused and was hearing someone she thought was me coming down the road. Until, that is, we slowly put two and two together.

We started realizing that when I spoke to Mom on the phone and she asked me what I was up to, the times I'd said I was just home were the same times that Moxy displayed the new behaviour. We decided to run some experiments and, sure enough, when I started calling Mom to signal that I was home (just letting it ring a couple of times to save money), it would be about five minutes after Mom would notice Moxy getting wound up. After racing around for a bit, by the time I'd call she was always settled back down and calm.

We figured out that Moxy was happy so long as she knew I was home safe, even if it was in another home and Moxy was signalling this to Mom so that she could stop worrying. It proved so accurate that from then on Mom just had to watch Moxy to know that I was home safe... but any ideas of staying out all night on the sly became a problem!

I was really excited by this story. I've heard of many cases of pets who seemed to know when their owners were coming home having been disproved or discredited by people saying that dogs have super-sensitive hearing and can hear and recognize their owner's car from miles away. In this case this wasn't what was happening at all.

Jodie's story

I got my cat Moyles when he was just a kitten and I was five years old. He grew into a big cat, but he was as soft as butter. Part Persian, ginger and white and very fluffy, he was a striking figure. That poor old cat used to get dragged everywhere with me. I used to dress him up in my doll's clothes and wheel him round in a pram. Luckily, he was a bit of a couch potato and so I don't think he minded that too much. But I guess he hated the way I scuppered his hunting instincts. He never had much luck tracking birds or mice as I was always hot on his tail. I used to take him to bed with me as well and cuddle him like a teddy. On reflection I did treat him a bit like a toy, which was rather unfair of me.

However, now that I recently started dating, Moyles is getting his own back. He's decided to become my 'boyfriend monitor'. Mum says maybe he can read auras or something, or maybe he just knows what *she's* thinking. I think that's more likely, because any time I bring home a boy Mum isn't going to like the look of, maybe a Goth or someone well-studded, or even one who's just a bit old for me, Moyles just won't have it. He hides behind chairs, which isn't easy for a big ginger-and-white fluff-ball, and leaps out as they're walking by, snaring them around the leg, scaring the life out of them and quite often sinking in his teeth or claws. It's weird, as he's usually such a gentle cat. Naturally, I don't see the boys he doesn't like for dust after that, and Mum just has this smug smile on her face. Maybe one day I'll bring someone home and Moyles will curl up on his lap – perhaps then I'll know who my husband is going to be, and so will Mum.

Now that I think about it, this kind of cat could be quite an advantage. Anyone who's had a string of disastrous relationships would find him very useful. Also, imagine in business if you could have your cat weed out the sheep from the goats, so to speak. It could save you a lot of money.

Jackie's story

I've never been in the slightest bit psychic and I was really a bit of a sceptic about the whole thing. I didn't even like horoscopes, so it never crossed my mind that a person and a dog might be able to communicate through thought alone – that all sounded a bit weird to me.

It all started one day when I went to collect my new puppy. He was a beautiful Weimaraner, a lovely 'ghost grey' colour. I'd fallen in love with him at first sight. Pal, as I called him, was my very first dog, and I was so proud and determined to do everything right for him. I read reams of books and made sure he had the perfect food, the perfect training, the perfect toys and bed – perfect everything, really, and he was, totally, the perfect dog. I knew (from all the books) that Weimaraners could be difficult to train, so I was sure to sign up for the top classes, and we started to become a brilliant team. Never having had a dog before, I hadn't realized how wonderful they are as companions. As Pal grew and we bonded, I started taking him for longer and longer walks, so I got fitter, too. We trekked across Exmoor and then finally across Dartmoor, and that was where it all came unstuck. The moors are huge, largely wild open spaces and, especially on Dartmoor, bad weather can close in really fast.

The only small issue Pal and I had was that he didn't always come when I called – or not immediately. It was just exuberance, but I'd been warned that one day it would get him into trouble, and it did. We were out on Dartmoor and we'd been walking for hours, stopping for lunch in the lee of a tor. I was just starting to think about how great it would be to get back to the place I was staying and sit down to a hot dinner. I'm sure Pal was dreaming of a warm bed by the fire, too. It was a nice day, really, cold but crisp, and of course we were very warm from all the exercise. We were probably only two miles from safety and warmth when it suddenly started to snow. At first it was pretty, but then it got really heavy and the wind blew, turning it into a blizzard. Before I knew it, I couldn't see the trail anymore and I only stayed safe because of my trusty compass, but Pal didn't know that. He started chasing the snow and got further and further away from me. His gorgeous colour didn't help as he blended in so well. I was trying to get him to stay close and then the worst thing happened, a rabbit – which had obviously been trying to pluck up the courage to make a break for home – shot out of cover right under Pal's nose. He chased after it, despite my screams to come back, and the two of them vanished into the whiteout. You can imagine the rest. I yelled and called myself hoarse, but Pal never came back. The snow got worse, the cold started to bite and I had no choice but to try and get back to the pub without my Pal.

I made it back, but I was desolate. I wanted Search and Rescue to go and look for my dog, but it was hopeless in the dark and, as they said, he could be miles away by then. After I'd spent a sleepless night, the day broke clear and the snow had stopped. I tried to find my way back to the spot where I'd lost track of Pal, but the snow had obliterated all the tracks. I stayed at the pub for two weeks in all, and every day I looked for Pal, but I never found a trace of him.

I cursed a friend who'd advised me not to get him micro-chipped, as she said some dogs were made ill by it. Everyone said I should give up on him, and that there was no way he'd ever find his way home from there. I went home, reluctantly, but Pal was never out of my thoughts for long. The worst thing was not knowing what had happened to him, and also blaming myself. If only I'd been a better trainer. If only we hadn't gone there that day. If only I'd had him micro-chipped, although that would only be any good if he turned up at a vet's and they checked for one. I'd been a bit of a loner before I got my dog, and now I was alone again. I got really depressed. Every evening when I went home from work I expected Pal to be sitting on the doorstep, but he never was.

Then, just when I'd given up all hope, I had a dream. I dreamed of Pal. He was in a big, cosy kitchen with a range. He was sitting up, not looking very relaxed, and whining. A woman appeared, and then, as Pal got up to greet her, I could see he had a heavily bandaged, maybe plastered, leg. I was so shocked I woke up. Could it possibly, possibly be that Pal had actually come to me in a dream? I didn't understand it, but I wanted to believe it more than I'd ever wanted to believe anything in my life. I decided to try the vets in the vicinity again. There were so many, because I had no idea how far Pal had roamed. I'd called all of the ones around where we'd been with no result, but then I decided to try something new. I sat down very quietly and cleared my mind. It wasn't easy, but then into my head popped a sign. It said, 'Tor Cottage'.

I was onto something, I just knew it! Have you any idea how many Tor Cottages there are in Devon? A lot! It took me several weeks of trying, phoning every post office in every village, but eventually I found him. A wonderful woman called Jean Nightingale had found my poor Pal the day after I'd lost him. He'd fallen off a rock in the snow and broken his leg.

I thank God every day that she found him, or he would have died for sure. Jean was happy to have the vet bills paid, and she was even happy to hand him back, because she said he had never been happy with her. I'll never know for sure what happened between me and Pal, but I know he looks at me kind of funny sometimes, and all but winks.

Pal's ability to connect with Jackie in dreams literally saved him. It's quite a remarkable tale. We all know that dogs can dream and are told that our dreams are just the sorting-through of the day's events, but I've never heard of a dog that could interact with his owner's dream before!

That amazing story of Pal finding a way to be reunited with his owner reminded me of what happened with our lovely cat, Felix. He was a wonderful, black, fluffy cat with the most vivid, big green eyes. He had a way of making his meow sound like 'Hello.' We had him for several years and then we moved house to a place out in the countryside. We had, of course, been warned that we mustn't let the cat out for several days, or we'd risk losing him for good. We had him shut in a basket for the actual move, but eventually we had to let him into the house.

Our son Phillip was only about seven years old at the time, and although we gave him strict instructions not to let Felix out, at his age he was so interested in running around in the new open spaces that he forgot. He opened the door without checking for the cat, after we'd only been there about five minutes, and whoosh, off went Felix, tail up, running for his life. He ran straight down the garden in the direction of the nearest road and vanished from sight. Phillip was crest-fallen so we made light of it, but Tony and I thought that was probably the last we'd seen of our cat.

Between the new house and the old house were about five miles of open fields, but there would also be several main roads to cross on the way. We decided that we'd give him a couple of hours and then drive back down there and see if there was any sign of him. I had a quiet few moments to pass in our new paddock, and I sat and thought about Felix. He'd been gone about an hour by then and I was tempted to go out in the car and look for him. Then I had a vivid mental picture of Felix trotting along a field edge, but ahead of him was the first of the main roads. I decided to try and capitalize on the connection, if that's what it was, so I started sending thoughts to Felix. I sent images of us, of a nice warm fireside and his food bowl. In my mind's eye the vision changed and Felix stopped trotting and stood still.

I then tried to show him all the mice and voles he'd be able to chase if he came back to our new place in the country, as opposed to his life in our previous, now barren town garden. I tried to communicate all the great adventures he could have in his new space and, in my vision, Felix turned around and started back the way he'd come. I was overjoyed as I really felt this was all real, and so I went back indoors and waited.

An hour later Felix came trotting back along the same path he'd bolted down two hours previously, and he never roamed far again.

Rachael's story

I was sitting with my little mini-foxy (Fox Terrier) Peanut, and was thinking about how guilty I was feeling about not walking her very much. I then thought to myself while looking at her, *What is it you would like to do today, Peanut?* I instantly saw a tennis ball flying through the air in my mind's eye and Peanut was wagging her tail and looking at me. I had to laugh out loud, as I knew how much she liked to retrieve the ball. I felt she'd communicated with me that she wanted to play fetch.

Rachael sent me this lovely little account from Australia and I think it's a fine demonstration of the close, everyday connection between some dogs and their owners.

The Barefoot Doctor's story

Walter was a dog with the most incredible charisma and air of intelligence. One look into those eyes was enough to make you understand that animals have souls that are, in many ways, more evolved spiritually than ours. He was a gorgeous champagne-coloured dog that was half-wolf, half-husky, and when he appeared on my TV show he was billed as 'Walter, the Almost-Human, Taoist Dog'. Despite his obvious great physical power, Walter was very gentle and cuddly, always keeping his great strength in check unless he needed it to defend himself.

Walter meted out doggie wisdom to my viewers and he was a very important part of my life. He never wore a lead and there was never any need. He patrolled his 'patch' in West Hampton with all the aplomb and assurance of a king.

The only time he got 'lost' was when I was in Spain. I can only imagine that Walter, back in England, was annoyed at my absence and thought he'd teach me a lesson by going walkabout. My poor PA, who was in charge of him at the time, was mortified at having to tell me she'd lost my dog, but after he'd been missing for 24 hours she rang me from the police station five miles from where we live, where she'd gone to report Walter missing.

I was a complete mess, but decided to try and connect with him and see if I could find out where he was. I went into a meditative state and summoned an image of my dog, asking him, 'Where are you? Come on, show yourself and let us know where you are.' The image of his face in my mind smiled, as only a dog can smile. The phone rang 10 minutes later. It was my PA. She could hardly speak because she was so dumbfounded. She told me that there she'd been, sitting in the police station, and Walter had just casually strolled in! He was filthy, with dirt and chewing gum and other unidentifiable gunge stuck in his coat, as if he'd been 'living rough', but apart from needing a bath, he was fine.

You have to ask yourself: how did he find her? How did he come to walk into that police station at that time? The only answer I can come up with is that he 'saw' the place by reading my mind and decided the time had come to turn himself in.

Please believe after reading this that any one of you can connect as deeply with your cat or dog. It just takes patience and practice and you don't have to be as spiritually attuned as the Barefoot Doctor to feel it. Your pet is spiritually attuned enough for both of you!

Alice's story

About 15 years ago we were gathering our six cats in carriers to take them to the vet's office for spaying and neutering. One of the males was an outdoor guy, and when my hubby went to find him he came back to the house with a beautiful calico female, asking me where she came from. Neither of us had ever seen her before. She was just as calm as can be as he held her. We put her in a carrier just to hold on to her while I phoned the neighbour. It turned out she was a stray who'd shown up at their place about a month before, and they didn't want her. 'Not cat-people', they said. That was fine with us. We took her to the vet's with the intention of keeping her.

When we brought the cats home from their ordeal I suggested we leave the new one in the carrier in the kitchen until she got her bearings. We called her Rosa, but since then we mostly call her 'Pootie' or Rosa MaCalico. I stayed around the kitchen that night and noticed that she just didn't seem bothered about being locked up at all. Even stranger, the other cats weren't curious about her. When I opened the door to her carrier, Rosa stepped out and stretched and then wandered into the utility room to use the litter box. She came back and went to the food and water and then onto the couch for a nap! Talk about making yourself at home! I felt like I knew her, and she was always looking at me. She's the only cat that I've ever encouraged to sit on the kitchen cabinet. If I was fixing the coffee pot, she'd watch intently, as if she were learning a new skill. She'd lean forward to smell the coffee when I took the lid off the can, then up straight again and watch the rest of the procedure.

I'd put a stop to allowing kitties in the bedroom after we got our new comforter. They were all young and picked at it until I thought we'd have feathers coming out. But, for some reason, we allowed Rosa in there. I loved being with her.

Now I have to fast-forward to two years ago. I always sleep on my side, and Rosa would always climb on my hip, lightly 'knead', and rest there awhile before settling on the bed against me to wash herself and curl up to sleep. It was almost like she was putting me to sleep first. She's real motherly towards the other cats, too. Two years ago this summer, though, Rosa started a rather bizarre behaviour. She'd get up on my hip as usual, but instead of lightly kneading right there, she'd reach down towards the bottom of my belly, closest to the bed. Balancing on my hip, she'd reach right down and actually pick at me through the covers. It didn't hurt so I'd let her carry on. Anyone who lives with and loves cats knows that if you stop them before they're finished with whatever's on their mind, they'll just keep going back to it until they *are* finished. Anyway, she kept on doing this every night.

I wasn't feeling real well that summer, and even made a doctor's appointment. I found out that I had a tumour the size of a tennis ball on my left ovary. Right there on the left side that used to be closest to the mattress, and right where Rosa had been picking at me. It wasn't until way after my surgery that I realized that Rosa's bizarre behaviour had stopped. It made me wonder. I do think that she was trying to help me and knew about that tumour. God, I wish they could talk – or even better, that I could listen and understand them more.

Rosa 'Pootie' MaCalico is still my 'baby'. Or is she my mother, come back to me? Most probably, in her next life, *she'll* be making the coffee.

I have no doubt that Rosa knew exactly what she was doing. Even cats that haven't been trained specifically can sense when something is wrong with their truly beloved owner. Pets this close to their owner are actually connected to them in a real sense, with a thread of energy, so they will be able to register untoward changes in cells. They will also sometimes attempt to heal those changes.

Steve's story

My twin brother and I are mediums, clairvoyant healers. My brother started to give readings before I did. One day he gave me a reading for our 22nd birthday. We sat in a bedroom with a candle between us and Chris used some Tarot cards. We had one of Mum's cats in the room, sitting quite happily under the table.

Chris was doing very well when we noticed the cat had seen something in the room. It chased around and around like there was an invisible mouse or something. The cat was literally going up the walls and over the bed and around and around in circles. This went on for a good couple of minutes when finally the cat became frightened of whatever it was and buried his head in my lap, so hard I thought it would hurt his face. He was shaking and just wanted to cover his head. I comforted him, which helped, but he stayed in that position for the rest of the reading. My trousers were covered in a mixture of cat saliva and hair. It was funny until he became frightened and then we asked whatever it was to leave. He eventually calmed down and acted all cool and cat-like, as though nothing had happened.

I remember reading that a cat's brain is made up of primarily optic nerve. I think that on that day this nerve was working a bit too well for Mum's cat.

If a photo had been taken during this episode, orbs may have appeared on the photos. Cats can often see what we cannot.

Ken's story

The cat that had most influence on me, and the one that I was closest too, was called Beano. We never discovered where he came from, either. I was already known by then as someone who would and could rehabilitate and rescue animals, so when a local woman found a five-week-old kitten, cold and hungry and sheltering in, of all places, a guard dog's bowl, she brought him to me. I couldn't resist. (How he didn't become the guard dog's dinner, I don't know.) We had to bottle-feed Beano to build up his strength; maybe that helped forge a strong bond. He was a gorgeous cat, a beautiful tortoiseshell with brilliant eyes. He would follow me all around the field while I tended our horses and sheep, and would run among our three dogs, tail aloft. When we took our pony and trap out he would occasionally hitch a ride to go sight-seeing around the village. Whenever I called him he would come as fast as the dogs did, and scamper straight up my leg and body to his customary perch on my shoulder. I loved that cat.

When we were forced to move from our small farm and go to the other side of the country, I didn't know what I'd do. We knew we'd be in rented accommodation for some time, possibly without a garden and possibly on a road, and we could just about sort the dogs out in that situation, but Beano was different. How could we expect a country cat, used to his own farm and his own eight-acre kingdom, to be happy in a rented house? We couldn't. But how could I leave him? It wasn't until our buyer for the property turned up that everything fell into place. He was walking around the yard, musing over whether to make us an offer, when up strolled Beano. With no introduction and no coaching from me, Beano ignored me and rolled upside-down on our visitor's shoe. It really was as if he knew. The gentleman immediately made an offer – on one condition. His purchase had to include the cat. Of course, I was really sorry to leave Beano; it almost broke my heart. But it was much better for him to stay where he could be happy and spoiled for the rest of his life, than for him to suffer with us, just to make me happy. I also believed that, as we were moving hundreds of miles away, Beano might do what I'd heard other cats had done and try to find his way home, but that because of the distance he'd never be able to do that. We sometimes have to be strong for our pets, don't we? The most compelling thing of all was that I believed Beano totally loved the new owner's energy, and that he did what he did quite deliberately because, of course, he had sensed we were going to say goodbye and he wanted to reassure me that he would be fine – and he was. Many years later I discovered that he had lived to a ripe old age and died naturally, after a long life of roaming the fields and bringing his owner 'little gifts'. Still miss that cat, though.

You might have found this story a bit sad until the end and wondered how Ken could ever have left his cat. But it turned out the cat was far more intelligent and knew exactly where he needed to be, and with whom, in order to have the best life he could.

Beverley's story

Like most people, our home has a special rhythm, which in our case starts about 6 a.m. My husband, Pablo, is the first to get up to turn on the coffee maker. While the coffee's brewing he greets the cats with a large can of cat food. Patches, the mama cat, is always served first and the 'kittens' show her fear and respect. Then they eat according to the pecking order. After they finish eating breakfast, they spread out to their favourite hunting spots to catch mice, squirrels, rabbits, snakes or birds, depending on the season. Next, a small herd of does, usually seven to nine, are waiting for their deer feed. Because the cats and the deer have grown up together, they naturally mingle together. By then the birds are anxiously waiting for the bird feeder and bird bath to be replenished. Of course, Pablo and I are last to be fed.

This everyday routine was shattered when tragedy struck one summer, as it became obvious that our beloved cats Brazos and Frio were nearing the end of their lives. Brazos and Frio were very close to each other, and to us. Although they were brothers, they couldn't have been more different. Brazos was a gorgeous long-haired yellow cat, quite big, with a big personality to match. Frio was solid black, long and lean with a cool, laid-back personality. Brazos and Frio loved to hunt together, cuddle with us and sleep together. They were especially close to Pablo. They always kept an eye on him, warned him of if there was a snake nearby and would cuddle in his lap at the end of the day.

When the boys were dying we made them as comfortable as possible. They were embracing each other as if they knew what was happening to them. My husband and I were spending as much time as possible with them yet also keeping up our daily routines. We were both crying as we watched the final moments of our precious kitties' lives. Brazos was the first one to die. When Pablo tried to remove him for burial, Frio held on to Brazos with all his might. Frio died the following afternoon.

This is when I realized how intertwined our lives are with our animals'. Even though everyone was fed as usual next day, all of the animals sensed that our 'rhythm' had been interrupted by great sadness. They saw us burying the boys and weeping at their graves. The deer reverently camped out in the front yard for three days, the cats sat on the patio and did not go hunting and the birds were unusually quiet. We were all in mourning together. And we were all meant to be together at that sad time in our lives. This is one reason why I am convinced that animals have souls.

Me too, Beverley! They have more empathy between them than people most of the time. We tend to think we're the most evolved species, but my life has taught me that, like it or not, in many ways our pets are more spiritually evolved than we are.

Alane's story

I like to feed stray cats. There is a stop on my 'feeding route', which I go to twice a week. It's one of many places where stray cats congregate. Sometime last year, a cat I dubbed 'Mildred' was in this little area of the woods where I keep bowls for food and water. She was a pretty little tortoiseshell, and I decided to take her to the free spay/neuter programme.

She was at my home recovering for a few days, then I was taking her back where I found her when a woman outside a nearby house said she owned the cat, and seemed very happy to have her back, saying that her boyfriend had brought her the cat from his job. She had been calling her 'Reesy', and thanked me for having her spayed, as they hadn't been able to afford it.

Unfortunately, over time I began to see more of the big picture. The women and her boyfriend appeared profusely drunk whenever I would pop in to feed that stop, and Mildred's food and water bowls were always empty.

The couple would be outside with company, in loud partying mode. Mildred would wander off, probably because of all the commotion. I found out that the woman had thought her boyfriend was bringing her a kitten from work, and she got Mildred instead, who was probably almost a year old. At some point I realized they'd moved. And I saw Mildred one day, confirming my worst fears that she had indeed been left behind.

I continued to feed her, but then she dropped out of sight for a very long time. A friend who helps me feed the stops told me on the phone one day that he'd seen a tortie come up. I instinctively felt this was Mildred. But then he said that her hair was coming out, and that she had a very tilted head. He'd given her some topical medicine at the time, for her skin.

When I was able to see her, some weeks later, I took her with me to have her checked out at my vet. I had no idea if anyone was caring for her. The vet examined her and said to try antibiotics for seven days for any lingering ear infection/vertigo problem, and then to take her back to her neighbourhood. A couple of days before it was time to return her, my friend called me from the feeding stop on his cell phone and said there was a woman there who was frantically trying to see about Mildred (or 'Snickerdoodle', which is what this woman had been calling her).

Apparently, she and her partner and little girl had welcomed Mildred into their hearts and home, and had been watching out for her as their own pet. The next time I went to go feed my stops, I took Mildred with me to have her big reunion with her new family. She'd tolerated being at my house, but I knew she'd be more comfortable in her normal surroundings.

There was the woman and her daughter coming out and smiling. I let Mildred out of the cat carrier and she trotted back and forth, taking it all in before she ran into the house.

I stayed to chat for a bit, then got ready to leave. Amid all the running about and taking in Mildred's return, there was a moment in time that had a profound impact on me. Mildred, aka Reesy, aka Snickerdoodle, interrupted her little rituals and came walking up to me. She tilted her head and lifted up a front paw delicately. She looked very, very intently into my eyes. It felt so intense that I was a bit startled, though of course I also felt touched and amused. She remained in this position for long enough of a pregnant pause that I said to the woman, 'I think she's trying to thank me for bringing her back!' I don't believe I've ever felt that strong a 'communication' with an animal before, and I won't ever forget it.

This appears just to be gratitude for Alane's kindness to Mildred, but I think it was more than that. Mildred brought a message to Alane from spirit to thank her on behalf of all the animals she has helped.

Madeleine's story

My youngest son was sitting at the table studying what looked like some very complex physics. I'd been a little concerned as to whether he was coping with his studies or not, but he hadn't mentioned anything so I hoped all was well. However, all of a sudden our lovely dog, Winnie, positioned herself under his chair and started to shake. She'd never done this before, so we felt alarmed. We thought she might be having a seizure. I asked her telepathically what was wrong, and I received a very clear message in my head from her saying, 'He's not happy and there's something he's not telling you!' I told my son what she'd said, but he just mumbled that he was fine. I replied, 'Well, Winnie isn't! And if you won't talk about it for my sake, tell me what the problem is so we can help Winnie to stop worrying about you!' He finally admitted that he was really struggling with his studies, but had been scared to tell anyone. As soon as he began to admit his problem, Winnie started jumping around wagging her tail. She seemed so relieved that she'd been able to bring this to light. My son and I had a lovely chat and he agreed to talk to his tutors and get extra tuition. As a result he did really well in his exams.

My son's far more open about telling me his problems now, as I only have to look at Winnie to know if anything's troubling him. She tells me if he's had a difficult day, or a headache. Whenever my son is out Winnie positions herself by the window precisely five minutes before he's due to return. He loves that she cares about him so much, and they're devoted to each other. Winnie also shares her loving care with some of my clients who come for healing and with the groups who attend my animal communication courses. I feel so blessed that our animals choose to share their lives with us and are so committed to helping us. They've been my greatest teachers.

I was lucky enough to know Winnie personally, and she really did have the softest energy. Sadly she is no longer in this world, but her legacy of love lives on.

Nina's story

When I was a young girl my father had a petrol station. Well, one night he came home with a German shepherd puppy. He said a man had stopped at the station for fuel and when my dad was filling up this man's truck he noticed a big sack in the bed of the vehicle, then all of a sudden the sack started barking! The man got out of the truck and told my dad he didn't want the puppy because her tail wasn't right, so he was going to throw her off a bridge. My dad grabbed the puppy and told the guy the next time he saw him he was going to throw him off the bridge. Of course, the puppy became ours.

We named her Kim, and had her for 14 wonderful years. All through her life she was incredibly intuitive, but there was one incident when she demonstrated this particularly well. It was several years after we got Kim, when my mother was stricken down with cancer and after a while she lapsed into a coma. My dad went to the hospital to see my mom one night while I stayed at home. All was quiet and then all of a sudden Kim started jumping around and barking. It wasn't like her at all, as she was usually very well behaved. She wouldn't leave my side for anything. She stared at the phone and I was shocked when it rang just as I looked at it. It was my dad, calling to tell me that my mom had passed. I told him I already knew and that Kim had told me. That was years ago, and Kim has gone to be with my mother. I often dream of them together, and know they're out there waiting. It makes my heart glad that to know that someday I'll be with them.

This dog waited to have a chance to replay the kindness she received from Nina's father and it finally happened. Dogs are sentient and situations like this prove their self-awareness.

John's story

A number of years ago I owned a Belgian shepherd called Rem. My work commitments meant he spent a great deal of time with my parents, in particular my mother. Then, one awful day, my mother was diagnosed with cancer. The treatment began in early January and was going well – until, that is, her kidneys failed. Unfortunately, she declined very quickly after that. I don't have any brothers or sisters, so I was at the hospital most of the time. However, I reached a point when I just had to come home for some rest, and left instructions that if anything were to happen, the hospital should contact me at once.

Around 1 a.m., Rem woke me up. He normally slept in my room and, although healthy, he was getting on in age, so at first I thought he simply needed to relieve himself. Out we went into the yard, but he just stood there for a moment, then turned and came back in. For the next 10 or so minutes he was very unsettled, pacing back and forth, crying and whimpering. I sat at the foot of the stairs with him for a while, and that's when I just knew what was wrong, so I went back upstairs to dress.

Shortly after this, I'm not sure of the exact time, the telephone rang and it was the hospital informing me that my mom had passed away shortly after 1 a.m. Once the phone call came, Rem became very quiet and settled down.

It's a night I'll never forget.

I was not surprised that Rem was able to sense the energy shift when John's mum passed away. Once he'd made John aware, he settled down because all animals know that death is not the end and that the person we feel is lost, is not lost at all, but just elsewhere.

CHAPTER 9

Strange Manifestations

There are some things we will never be able to explain, as the universe is a mysterious place with so much about it unknown by us. Some strange events involve our dogs and cats, and there are many theories out there as to what it all means. Relationships between species tend to strengthen my already strong belief that dogs and cats (and other animals) do come back to us, sometimes in very strange ways, sometimes as the same species they were before, sometimes as other animals and sometimes as people. Or another explanation, preferred by some people, is that the souls of our loved ones, human or animal, can sometimes momentarily share the body of another living being to send us a message or share a soul either permanently or temporarily (but always with the consent of the primary soul).

There was a woman out there a year or two ago who was making a wonderful living claiming that she could bring a dead pet's soul back to life by 'hi-jacking' another animal's soul. In other words, if you had lost a dog or cat, she would encourage you to buy or home another one, and then she would claim to have inserted the soul of your lost pet into it. That was abhorrent to me, as I'm sure it is to you, too. Thankfully, she now seems to have disappeared. I am a firm believer that everyone is entitled to their own theories and opinions, but that we must never harm another soul deliberately and that each being's soul is sacrosanct.

There are times when a soul, animal or human, will allow another soul to use them in order to reach out to someone, but it's all purely voluntary and 99.9 per cent of the time it's temporary, too.

To follow are some fabulous stories describing unique working and spiritual partnerships that evolve between us and a cat or a dog. Other stories remind me that we are all mystical beings, and sometimes we should not even bother trying to figure everything out, but just accept the wonderful gifts our pets bestow upon us. Whatever way you look at it, we are all connected on a soul level – and that is the most important thing to remember.

Lara's story

I am an Angelic Reiki Master and in my practice I offer angel treatments as well as Angelic Reiki workshops. I'm also the proud owner of Minnie, a nine-year-old tabby kitty cat that has been with me and my family since when she was a baby. Having been born at the RSPCA from a rescued mother, she had nowhere to go and was likely facing a sad fate, had she not been adopted. I picked her up from the sanctuary on the day of my 40th birthday, as a special treat to celebrate my life milestone. I'd had cats before, but this was the first one I'd owned with my new husband and in our new house. All so very exciting! From day one Minnie proved to be a great addition to the family, so affectionate and generally well behaved with both adults and children, with just the occasional grumpy moment if disturbed when resting.

During the next two years after her arrival, I qualified as an Angelic Reiki Master and started treating clients and teaching students this marvellous technique that relies on the energy of angels to facilitate healing. As I was studying, I used to practise often on myself and on friends and family as part of my apprenticeship.

Soon I started noticing that, whenever I ran an Angelic Reiki session, Minnie would promptly appear out of nowhere and sit in the room. This has not stopped since and to this day, every time Angelic Reiki is involved, she comes flying.

At the beginning, she used to just sit close to me when I was self-treating, then one day she physically placed herself under my hand as I was treating myself and that's when I understood that the wanted some of that beautiful energy, too. From that day, I started to treat her on a regular basis and she became one of my case studies. A while after completing my qualification, I ran my own Angelic Reiki course for the first time and as I gave the attunements to my students, Minnie the kitty cat appeared from thin air and sat in the circle with us. The attunements are the rituals by which the Master imprints the symbols on the students and so initiates them to allow the flow of Angelic energy to run through their bodies. It is a transformational process that I believe brings us closer to angels.

From that moment, every time I ran a course, Minnie wanted to be part of it, sitting in the room and enjoying the vibe. Still to this day, she sits in front of me and constantly looks at me as I speak, listening intently, and if I forget a topic, she promptly meows in protest or even discretely attracts my attention to my notes! Lately, I have noticed that she has also started yawning when I go on a little too much on a single topic, and that's my cue that I need to wrap it up and move on to the next part of the course, so that I can give the right amount of time and attention to the whole programme.

When I have a client for an Angelic Reiki treatment, Minnie does the 'meet and greet' service, sniffing, rubbing and purring as I conduct the routine initial consultation. She seems to know who to approach and who not to, and the other day she sat on the other side of the treatment room without approaching a lady at her first appointment. I started to wonder what was wrong with her or with the client, only to discover a few minutes later that the client is allergic to cats. Did Minnie know? I think she didn't, but she must have been told by angels to stay away from the lady for medical reasons.

When I give an Angelic Reiki treatment, Minnie sits in the room and stares at me, observing all my movements. She is usually quiet and relaxed, but on occasions she starts licking her body, furiously insisting on the same point. The first few times this happened, I didn't make much of it, thinking that it was just strange behaviour from my strange cat and left it at that. With time, however, I realized that there was a correspondence between the areas of the body that Minnie was so desperately licking and the areas of concern in the body of the client. So, I understood what she was trying to do. My cat was showing me where the issue with the client was and therefore where my healing efforts needed to be concentrated. I normally came to the same conclusion as Minnie, but I must admit that at times she is quicker than me! That's not surprising, thinking about it, as cats are less rational than us humans and therefore more open to intuition and angel energy.

I'm always amazed to see the work of God through angels in everyday life and, if that means that a kitty cat is turned into an Angelic healer to better help clients, I am grateful that that cat is my Minnie!

This cat takes sensing and healing illnesses to a whole new level! I feel she must have already lived as a human to have learned the knowledge to be able to work in this way.

Sarah's story

I have two daughters, Megan and Lauren, and they had both been nagging me for a very long time to get a pet. Megan was keen on having a hairless cat and Lauren just wanted anything really.

Lauren is quite a sensitive soul, very compassionate, and she would get upset sometimes because she wanted a pet so much. She was beginning to ask me daily to get one and although there was a part of me that wanted to give in, I kept thinking about the commitment, time and money, especially if we had a dog.

After weeks of Lauren getting upset, I reached out to the angels one day. I just said if it's meant to be, then please put a pet for Lauren in my path, one that will cost me no money to buy, one that I don't have to go looking for – if it's meant to be for Lauren to have a pet, it will appear in my path.

A week later, an email came from my mum's workplace with the subject line 'Home me'. Mum said that there was a girl in her office whose brother's cat had a litter of kittens and there were only two left, both boys. If they didn't get a home that day, they were being given to the cat and dog home. After thinking for about five minutes, I decided to take them both. I absolutely couldn't believe it. Not only had these pets appeared in my path without me even looking for them, but there was one for each of my daughters.

By 6 p.m. that night, they had arrived at the house. I didn't tell Lauren they were coming and her face was a picture when she saw them. She first thought we were only looking after them, but when she realized they were staying, her little eyes welled up with tears. The odd thing is, when we put them down on the floor, one went to Megan and one went to Lauren and that was how they decided who was having whom. Megan called her one Oreo and

Lauren called hers Olaf. They are almost six months old at the time of writing and as they've grown and their personalities have formed I could swear that they have been here before. I have this strange feeling that Oreo is a dog of ours called Sam who died last September, and Olaf was a beloved cat of mine called Phoenix, who died aged two, 17 years ago.

I have a set of angel cards and Lauren likes to pick a card now and again. Ever since we got the cats Lauren has said that she knows what they are thinking, that she can communicate with them. Today she picked a card that told her she had a very strong bond with her pets, and that animals respond to her kind and gentle ways. It said that her pets on Earth are surrounded by angels and that she is able to communicate wordlessly with them.

I do believe that these cats are a very special gift from the angels for us. I feel something very strong when they look at me and they have brought so much happiness, joy and laughter to our home.

This wonderful story illustrates the innate and natural connection between children, animals and angels. All three energies have combined together to create a wonderful mode of communication between species.

Cathy's story

My cat, Bronson, was a tough guy, but he was very kind and healing, too. I had two cats at the time: one was Georgie, a Ragdoll that never went outside (he wasn't street-wise), and Bronson, who was the opposite, and would disappear for days on end doing goodness knows what. He was the epitome of independent! But, if ever I felt unwell, Bronson would give up his roaming ways instantly, as if he knew, and appear at the door, mewing as he negotiated the cat-flap. Then he would come and sit right beside me. This was very important to me because I'm epileptic and live alone apart from my cats.

When he was 14 years old Bronson disappeared and, unlike previous times, he didn't come back, ever. I never knew what had happened to him. Well, that's not quite true, as I did know that he had been killed or had died, because I still felt him next to me whenever I felt unwell. This always warned me that I was going to have a seizure.

Feeling his presence wasn't the end of it either. As I got older, I was less able to take care of myself when my illness got the better of me and I needed more help. At this point you'll have to suspend your disbelief because I have trouble believing it myself. I have two close friends and neighbours, Chris and Paul. Both of them have at times come rushing into my house in the middle of the night, just as a seizure started, and told me that they did so because they dreamed about Bronson, that he was on their bed, pawing at their face until they woke up. I honestly believe I owe Bronson my life several times over.

Such a clever cat! Obviously he's an old soul, even able to astral-travel to appear in the dreams of Chris and Paul. Amazing!

Diane's story

Many of my dogs and cats have special needs, like my cat Stevie, who was born without eyes, and was found sleeping in the middle of the street. He changed my life. He showed me what I am. Sadly, he's no longer with me.

Stevie was and still is the only true love of my life. No family member, friend or even any other fur-baby can compare. On the fateful day when I had to let him go, I held his head gently in my hands as the vet set him free from his ailing body. As I did so, Stevie turned his head towards me, like he had eyes and was 'looking' into mine. It was as if he were seeing me for the first time – and then he was gone. Once the vet had taken his body away, I went home and cried. I remembered all he had shown me during our time together. I recalled all the times we would lie together, breathing as one, his paw in my hand, both of us in an almost meditative state.

Then one day I had a vision of him and I saw myself with him, but in this vision I didn't have two legs, I had four. I was a cat. I could see my four legs, stomach and part of my back. I watched Stevie and I walking together, seeing other cats and greeting them as cats do, with a head bump and by sniffing each other. I saw people pick me up. I believe I really and truly was seeing us together in another life when we were both cats.

I'm sure we all have déjà vu experiences, but when I have them they're not from the standpoint of a human, but from the perspective of a cat. It's hard to describe, but Stevie opened my eyes to my past. It's my firm belief that I was once a cat, and in my human life now I can communicate with them in ways that others don't understand. I know now why Stevie and I were so close – we'd been together before.

This story shows that not all 'seeing' is done with the eyes. Stevie was obviously a dab hand at reading energy with his 'third eye', that invisible psychic lens that we all have in the centre of our foreheads. I loved this story because, while I have many about people owning the same pet before in other lives, I've not come across a person and a cat that were cats together before.

Julia's story

We used to have two little dogs. Our Yorkie was called Matilda and our poodle was called Demi, and they were totally devoted to each other. When little Matty (Matilda) died I don't know who grieved more, us or poor Demi. We didn't think she could understand, but she watched as we buried our little girl next to the apple tree in the back garden. She'd watched over Matty whenever she was sick, and so every day she'd take one of their soft toys, a furry rabbit, and place it next to Matty on her bed. Matty never played with the toy, although it had always been her favourite, so we took it away each day so Demi wouldn't be upset that her gift had been ignored.

A few days after she had died, I went to Matty's grave to make sure weeds weren't growing there. (I planned to plant a nice little rose, but it was the wrong time of year yet for it to be flowering.) I was amazed to see the furry rabbit toy sitting there right in the middle of the grave. I thought one of the kids, or Robert, my husband, must have put it there, but no one had. It had to have been Demi. To me this totally proves that Demi did love her little friend and that dogs do have souls.

How utterly beautiful that Demi gave her little friend the only gift she had to give.

Charly's story

My cat Winter is a Turkish Van. He's mostly white with a darker Siamese-like mask, dark tail and piercing blue eyes. True to his breed, he's incredibly smart, regal, savvy and (unlike many cats) he loves water, which is a Turkish Van trait.

My favourite story is of our initial meeting. I was living in Los Angeles, dealing with the red tape involved in trying to find a kitten. I wanted a very special cat with a very special connection, and I believed I would know when I found him. LA cat shelters had all kinds of ridiculous rules that made the entire process a struggle, so my husband at that time, who was in Wisconsin, suggested I get a kitten from there instead, the next time I was visiting him. So I went along to the Spooner Humane Society, as I've supported them in the past. Inside there were lots of options, but none that had that extra special something I was looking for. Before arriving, I had really felt that my cat would be there, so I was definitely feeling disappointed when I left.

As I started to make my way out, the manager came from the back and asked if I'd seen the kittens that were in quarantine. She said there were only a couple, but they'd just come in and so they needed to stay separate to ensure their health and that of the other cats in residence. We opened the door, I looked to my left and there I saw my beloved (then unnamed) Winter, rolling and wrestling with another kitten.

The manager said the other kitten was his sister, but I remember feeling such an incredible difference between the two. Winter's white coat was so beautiful that I just watched him for a minute. He had such feistiness, I could just tell he was a rascal and not the kind of cat who would run and hide when people came over. So as he rolled over I leaned in towards the cage and said, 'Are you the one? Are you supposed to be my cat? Am I supposed to bring you home with me?' Just then he suddenly got up from his play, walked to the edge of the cage and stood eye to eye with me. He slipped his tiny little paw through the cage and rested it gently against my cheek. He even let me touch it before pulling his paw back into the cage, then he just stood there as if he knew something had been accomplished. The manager just about passed out at the sight of such a thing, as she said she'd never seen anything like it. She kept saying, 'Oh my, he has definitely chosen you!'

Of course, I was thrilled, and gave her strict instructions to keep him safe for me and not show him to anyone else, as I would be coming back for him the next week. I flew back to LA, then a week later I drove from California back to Wisconsin to get him. It was December when I picked him up. Then I drove down through Minnesota, Iowa and Nebraska down into New Mexico, where I spent Christmas. Next stop was Las Vegas, where I visited with my parents and Winter met the family dog for the first time. They became incredibly fast friends! California was our last stop. Winter has been an amazing addition to my life ever since. Now five years old, he's the only cat I know who gets invited to dinner parties and ladies' luncheons. I keep him on a strict healthy diet, but he does take his place at dinner tables and conversation pits when we entertain or visit friends. Everyone marvels at his intelligence.

One has to wonder if Winter has spent a previous life as some kind of raconteur or entertainer, because he's certainly stepped very easily into that role.

Lynn's story

Tiger was my first ever cat and she was a tabby. My mother got her for me and my sisters. She was a lovely, lively cat when she wanted to be and would bring us gifts – birds and mice mostly. I was two years old when we got her and we grew up together. There was always a bond between us. I loved the dogs we had as well, but Tiger was my cat.

She went missing at one point and I was devastated, but I just knew she wasn't gone forever. I prayed for her to come back to us, and two weeks later as my mum was coming home with the shopping, she heard a familiar meowing coming from a boarded-up house at the bottom of the road. My grandad got a crowbar and made a gap large enough for us to see inside and for Tiger to escape, and out she popped. She was starving, but well apart from that. From then on our bond got even stronger.

When I became a teenager she would lie curled up on my bed next to me as I listened to Spandau Ballet, my favourite band at the time. It was also Tiger's favourite. If I put any other band on my stereo, her tail would start twitching. When Spandau Ballet's song 'True' would come on, her tail would curl under her and she would start purring contently. No one believed me when I said that it was her favourite song.

One Bank Holiday Monday we were all sitting in the living room, listening to the radio. We were relaxed and Tiger was curled up in front of the fire. The Bee Gees song 'How Deep Is Your Love?' came on. It starts a little bit like 'True' and I noticed Tiger move slightly, so I watched her. She started purring. At this point I said to everyone 'Tiger thinks this is Spandau Ballet's 'True'.' I was told not to be so stupid, but we all started watching her. When she realized it wasn't her favourite song after all, she stopped purring and her tail started twitching violently in annoyance. At this my mum just looked open-mouthed, and my eldest sister said, 'Oh, my word, she *does* only like that song!' We all started laughing, but this annoyed Tiger even more. I apologized to her and scooped her up in my arms. But even that didn't make her happy. So I realized what I had to do. I carried her upstairs to my room and placed her on my bed, put my stereo on and played her 'True'. As I sat back on the bed she rubbed up against me, purring, then curled up into a ball with a contented look on her face. When the song finished her tail started twitching so I had to put it on again – and again and again until she was asleep. My sisters came up to see how she was and just shook their heads in disbelief. When she finally fell asleep I went downstairs, only for my sisters to accuse me of brainwashing the poor cat into liking the song.

Tiger went on to live until she was 20 in human years. I was heartbroken when she died, but every time I hear that song I think of Tiger and smile.

This was not only Tiger's favourite song but one that she felt was 'their' (Tiger and Lynn's) song. Couples have songs they call 'theirs', so why not this kind of partnership, too?

John's story

Jiminy the Whippet was named after the Walt Disney cricket, as he had extra-long back legs that would fold up under him when he sat, and then he'd bounce straight up into the air, come down, spin round and do it again. I rescued him when he was two years old – I couldn't help it really, as although he had no less than eight other dogs in with him, his leaping up and down high above their heads soon brought him to my attention.

It became obvious pretty quickly that Jiminy loved most people and I soon decided that he should become a 'PAT' dog. Any breed of dog or cat can become part of a PAT team. But they must have been with their owner for at least six months, be over nine months old and pass the assessment. They will then be trained to visit residential homes, hospitals, hospices, schools, day care centres and prisons. Jiminy was perfect. He flew through the assessment, and his forte turned out to be hospices and care homes. I soon found out why he was most welcome in those places. He would come round with me, giving each and every patient his utmost attention, sitting as long as necessary to accept any cuddles and endearments that were offered. He just seemed to have real empathy with very old and or ill people. He knew just how long to stay with them without tiring them, and who needed an extra bit of his attention on any particular day. Occasionally he would climb on someone's lap and let them hug him tight, and the nurses or staff would tell me that that person had been a bit down before our visit, but they always perked up after a Jiminy special cuddle.

But the weirdest thing was that he always insisted on one last look at everyone before we left. And not only that, I soon noticed that when it came time to leave he would always manage to make me go to whichever person he wanted me to take him to last, to say goodbye. And you've probably guessed it, that person would soon pass away. In fact, they were always gone the next time we went. I never told anyone my suspicions, that somehow he knew, but I'm sure he did. He was always subtle, so the residents and patients never realized what was going on, but I knew.

I suspect Jiminy must have had a human life in which he lived until he was very old. Maybe that gave him an extra rapport with people who are now in that same position. He would also have been reassuring them that it wouldn't be the end when they passed.

CHAPTER 10

Dogs and Cats That Send Us Another Pet

This is probably going to be my favourite chapter! I really have lost count of the times I have comforted someone who has lost a pet by telling them that if the bond was really so strong, their pet will have the option to come back to them, and if they aren't able to do that for whatever reason, they will inevitably direct the owner to a new pet they have chosen for them or even sometimes direct a new pet right to the owner.

Most devoted dog or cat owners resist getting a new pet when they've lost one, sometimes for months, sometimes for ever. They feel that to switch affection is some sort of betrayal to the pet they lost. But this really isn't the case. Animals are incredibly unselfish in this regard and will guide their owners, if allowed, to another dog or cat that desperately needs a home of the kind they themselves enjoyed. They do not begrudge another pet that chance. They really do want every other cat and dog to have what they had. You must look for the signs and accept them if they come. If they do, you won't be left in any doubt. If you lose a pet that was your best friend and had a really special link with you, so that you want them to come back, and yet worry that you might miss them if they do, then don't worry, there will be some sort of definite signal that they're the right one for you.

Sue's story

A few years ago I was feeling devastated because my dad had passed away unexpectedly. I thought I'd never get over it, but then I had a fantastic dream about him. He said that he was with my old dog, Juno, a Great Dane, who had died a while before. He told me that Juno was going to come back to me, to help me get over losing him (my dad). He described Juno's unmistakable blue merle colour and then showed me an altogether different dog, which was an all black, Labrador cross collie. He told me Juno was coming back as a smaller, plainer dog, to fit in with me better and make him easier to lift! I remember almost waking at that point, a little chuckle on my lips, as I recalled the times I had tried unsuccessfully to lift Juno's mighty bulk into the car. I also remembered with sadness how short-lived the big breeds are and how I'd lost Juno when he was only six years old. A smaller breed would at least live longer and that made me happy!

Then my Dad told me that the new dog was going to come to me from the Mattishall Road. This worried me and for the next several weeks as I drove my regular route to work I was watching out for a dog on the road, ready to stop the car and grab him before he could get run over. It was a fast road with blind bends and it could easily have happened. After those few weeks I still believed, but felt I was already getting too attached to a dog I hadn't even yet met, and that I would be heartbroken if he didn't appear. I started to think the dream had just been a dream.

Then I had another dream – a lot shorter as if Dad had better things to do! He just stayed long enough to tell me that Juno was coming back as Mickey. When I woke up I was mystified as I don't think I would ever have chosen that name for a dog. I would have gone for something more like Zeus!

Anyway, angels work in strange ways because a week later a work colleague asked me if I'd heard about the puppy that had been picked up on a road near me. She said it was black and had been taken to the local dog shelter. Could it be the dog from my dream? Of course, I had to go there to see, and sure enough they had a puppy that a member of the public had brought in from Mattishall Road. I took one look at his big, round, stick-up ears and said, 'Mickey!' The puppy came rushing across to me and sat, bolt upright, as if saying, 'Yes! Are you here for me at last?' The woman there was amazed, saying they had nicknamed him Mickey because they thought he looked like Mickey Mouse. Mickey is sitting at my feet right now. Whenever he's near me I feel calm and peaceful, and hopeful for a future I thought had died with my Dad.

Angels certainly do work in strange ways. It's as if it rarely is simple, and there are always complexities that we have to go through to get to where we're meant to be. I think they're a kind of a test, but also lessons in learning to trust and to listen.

Kathleen's story

Mork, my special cat, came to me as the lone survivor of a litter of kittens. He seemed to be imbued with an especially strong connection to life, for he survived the loss of his mother and all of his litter-mates by the time he was just two weeks old. I bottle-fed him after his mother passed on, took care of all of his needs and he survived against all odds. Perhaps the bond between us was established at this time. He became more like a child than a pet, and even my children to this day think of him as being more like a brother.

His life was nearly taken from us so many times during the 18 years we were together. He got in a scrap with another cat, perhaps a feral animal, which left him with a raging infection that nearly took his life. I nursed him through that. One fateful day years later I rescued Mork from the jaws of a neighbour's dog. He was so severely injured (internally nearly bitten in two) that he had to have extensive surgery after a frantic rush to the emergency vet through a snow storm. He miraculously recovered. Some years later I found him out in the garden in a secluded spot very near death's door. I scooped him up and took him to the veterinary hospital. The diagnosis was severe anaemia. I took the poor half-dead fellow home. He was so near death that his body temperature was low and he was semi-conscious and delirious. He very nearly passed away that night. I sat up with him all night long, keeping him warm and hydrated, and when morning came I knew my efforts were not futile because he wasn't in renal failure! He got up and promptly peed on my basket of clean laundry. I was overjoyed! Life settled down for a few years after that and we enjoyed Mork's older years with us.

One day the vet told me that Mork's kidneys were failing. I asked if they did kidney transplants on cats. It might sound silly, but Mork was like my child and I would have done anything to keep him living as long as possible. The vet told me they didn't do them. (Shortly after this, veterinary medicine made advances in that area. Too late for my Morkey, though.) We faced the inevitable and about a year after the dire prognosis Mork's kidneys indeed began to fail. He passed quietly in my bedroom and we buried him in a prominent spot in the garden near the front door.

His passing left a big hole in our family. We'd got a kitten shortly after getting the dire prognosis of kidney failure for Mork. We'd named the new kitten Korkey. She was an orange long-haired cat similar to Mork, and she was charming and sweet, but somehow not enough to fill the void left by Mork.

A couple of years passed and we started to get the feeling that we needed to get a small companion dog. We spent months researching the breeds of dogs that would suit our needs, and we settled on either a Pug or a Boston Terrier. While driving one day we passed a pet store and saw a sign outside that said, 'Puggleys'. 'Puggley? What is a Puggley?' we asked each other. So we turned the car around and went back to find out what a Puggley was.

We went in and saw a small fellow in a cage. He looked a little like a tiny brown bear. It was love at first sight. This was a pet shop where I had stopped many, many times over the years to look at the pups. I had never been tempted to buy before – I never considered buying a dog from a pet shop like this, which might for all I knew be getting pups from a puppy farm. So we went home without the little brown bear-doggy, but he was on my mind the whole night. I insisted we go back and see if he was still there the next day and, by morning light, I was determined that the little fellow would be mine.

I brought him home and sent out an announcement and a photo telling everyone we had a new family member. Several people asked, 'What is it?' I looked at the photo and had to admit he was a nondescript sort of creature. I realized that in the photo he looked like very much like a kitten, so I had to send another note explaining that we had got a puppy. We named him Zammis.

He immediately bonded with me and he very soon had me running him to the vet with an emergency – just like old times. I began to notice Zammis' mannerisms resembled Mork's.

He would sit with his back to me just like Mork did, like he was guarding me. The colour of his fur (the under coat) was similar to the colour of Mork's fur. Mork had been perhaps part Maine Coon and he had a bit of a mane around his head and neck, and so did Zammis. And then there were the tortilla crisps. Mork had been a fanatic for corn tortilla crisps. If I was eating them he would jump up in my lap and snatch them right from my hand as I was about to put them in my mouth. Zammis began doing the same thing. Zammis is always there as soon as he hears me munching on tortilla crisps and insists on getting a crisp in very much the same way Mork did.

Zammis seems to have many cat-like traits. He also had a sweet relationship with Korkey who was here as Mork grew old. Korkey welcomed Zammis without any cat versus dog conflict. I used to catch them relaxing on the bed together, with Korkey stretching out, reaching paw to paw as if she recognized that Zammis was a cat, too.

I now have seven dogs and I have had many cats over the years, but my relationship with Mork was so different to all the others and so special, and my relationship with Zammis feels so much the same. I do feel a special soul connection with them. I can't say for sure that they are the same soul, but I have a strong feeling that Mork is with me still and always will be.

Zammis may have been one of those rare partnerships I mentioned where one soul will voluntarily accept a snippet of another soul into their body envelope in order to help a much-loved owner. In that way the rest of the 'stowaway' soul can go off in some other direction it needs to, while not totally abandoning their previous owner.

Petra's story

I loved my cat Darley, and when he got ill when I was about 14 years old, I would sit for hours rocking him on my lap and trying to will him to get well, even though everyone said it was useless. We'd got Darley when I was less than a year old, and Mum had named him after the Darley Arabian, as she loved horses and liked the name. She told me that some people told her to keep him away from the baby (me) when she first got him, in case he suffocated me by sitting on my face or scratched me, but she didn't take any notice and Darley never hurt me. He would practically babysit me. In fact, he used to go and get her if he heard me crying. When she took me out for a stroll in the pram she said he would often walk alongside, and if he got fed up she'd let him sit beside me in the pram. She got some really funny looks when people asked if they could see the baby and found the two of us in there staring back at them! I grew up with my cat and I took him places most people would say you can't take cats. Of course, there wasn't too much traffic about in those days. You probably couldn't do it now. He was my pal.

When he got ill I hoped and prayed he'd get better, but sadly he didn't. He died and we buried him in the garden, said our goodbyes and I made a little cross to put there. For months people tried to encourage me to get another cat, but I didn't want another cat, I just wanted my friend back again. In the end, though, Mum got worried about how depressed I was getting at such a young age, and she came home one day with a little jet black kitten from the cat rescue centre. Choosing this colour was a good move because Darley had been pure white, so it didn't look like she was trying to replace him, as that would not have worked. After a while I couldn't resist the little black kitten, but that didn't stop me feeling really guilty. My mum couldn't understand why I wouldn't take the new boy, Jackson, up to bed with me like I had Darley. I hadn't told her that every night I could still feel Darley jump on the bed and feel his vibrating purr as he cuddled up. I was afraid that if I took Jackson up, Darley would be upset and stop visiting me.

One night the kitten made it upstairs by himself, and before I knew it he was up there on the bed. I was about to do a really nasty thing and chuck him off, but then I felt it, the purring. It was like Darley was curled up against me. But then something really weird happened: Jackson rolled on his back, displaying his tummy in submission, and I could actually see the hairs of his coat being flattened as if by an invisible tongue, as if Darley was licking him. I could distinctly hear two purrs; it was an amazing sound. That night I slept with Jackson curled up next to me. I didn't mind that afterwards I never felt or heard Darley again, because I knew the new boy had his approval. A pet psychic even told me that Darley might have put his soul, or part of it, into Jackson. I liked that idea.

Darley was a pet that for some reason couldn't return to his owner, so he brought Jackson in to take his place. No wonder he pulled out all the stops to make Petra realize that she had to accept him!

Edwina's story

Our dog Brandi was a wonderful little dog. She was very gentle and full of love. It soon became apparent, however, that she had one very dangerous weakness. She loved to climb fences. We'd never seen anything like it! She would shin up a fence more like a cat or a fox than a dog. We started watching her carefully when she went out, and the rest of the time she stayed in the house. After a couple of years my husband and I divorced, and my girls and I moved to a tiny apartment. We left Brandi and our other dog with my ex-husband, who promised to take care of them.

One afternoon as I was driving downtown, I saw a very frightened large dog running along the sidewalk, obviously lost. I stopped to help. The dog turned out to be an adult Doberman that had obviously recently had puppies. She was very glad to see a friendly face and came to me happily and sweetly. I decided that the best thing would be to take her to our local animal shelter. I couldn't take her home and I knew they would have the best chance of reuniting her with her puppies. When I was leaving the shelter I suddenly felt compelled to return back to the building and as I approached one of the kennels, my heart leapt into my throat. There was Brandi! She'd been injured and couldn't walk. My ex-husband had neglected to tell me that she had got out and not returned home. I was furious!

Brandi had been hit by a car and the vet said she'd broken her back. She didn't appear to be in any pain, but she'd never walk again and wouldn't be able to control her bodily functions or do anything for herself. My family faced an agonizing decision, but in the end we decided that the kindest thing was to let Brandi go. It was so hard to do.

After a couple of days I thought again of the Doberman. If it hadn't been for her, I'd never have found Brandi. Even though it wasn't a happy ending, at least she got to spend her last days with the family who loved her, and that was a precious gift. I called the shelter to check on the Doberman, and she had indeed been claimed and was home with her puppies. I believe in my heart that she was Brandi's guardian angel, sent from heaven to guide me to where I needed to be. For that, I am grateful.

Aren't animals wonderful when they help each other out like this?

Jacqui's story

I used to have a lovely red boxer called Sophie. When she passed I was heartbroken, as she'd never left my side when she was alive. I belonged to a psychic development circle, and I was delighted that after she died Sophie appeared there many times. One special evening I received an image of her placing a small red puppy on my lap. My first instinct was 'Oh no!' I'd decided that I couldn't go through the heartache of loss again, and I wouldn't have another dog no matter what. But then out of the blue a boxer breeder I knew rang me up and asked if I wanted a rescue puppy. We were about to go on holiday so I said I'd give her my answer when I got back.

While I was away I decided not to have the rescue puppy, and so I rang the breeder when I got back to tell her, but fortunately the puppy had already been re-homed. The breeder went on to say that her own boxer had just had a litter, and without thinking I said, 'If there's a red female, she is mine.' I have no idea what made me say that. A sudden image of Sophie and a red puppy? It was agreed and, of course, there was a red puppy in the litter, so along came Lucy.

One morning when I was out walking Lucy, she ran into some woods, and when I called her to come back, I clearly saw two red boxers emerging from the trees, but when Lucy reached me she was alone. That evening I went to my psychic circle and the medium said she had a message for me. She told me it didn't make sense to her, but was simply, 'And then there were two.' It made perfect sense to me – Lucy had been running in the woods with Sophie's spirit.

It's really good when we get a strange message like this that no one else but us would understand. It really does prove that the message is real.

Edward's story

Chipper was my best buddy for 16 years. He was called Chipper because he was such a happy little guy, but also because he was found in the timber yard where I worked – he was nearly lopped in half by a circular saw, but seen just in time. He was ginger with black dots strategically placed all over him. Two of them made a cute moustache. He came everywhere with me in my truck, and there were times when he was more like a dog than a cat. He would guard the truck, leaping ferociously at the window if anyone came too near when I was out of the vehicle. When he passed away I missed him so much. I would have got another pet, maybe a dog this time, so I didn't feel too much like I had betrayed him, but I just knew that if it wasn't the same sort of companion Chipper had been I wouldn't have really loved it and that would have been mean.

I'd retired by then – no more wood yard – and I had a lot of time on my hands, so I started helping out with the ASPCA and qualified as a part-time inspector. It was a tough job, seeing animals that had been ill-treated and learning that though we tried to help and re-home them, sometimes the kindest thing was to let them go painlessly. I never felt like homing any of them myself, because they weren't Chipper. Cute little kittens and puppies held no sway over me.

But then I started to realize that I had a real affinity for the old ones. I used to feel so bad for them. A lot of them had enjoyed a good life, loved and cossetted, until their later years when their owner died or went into a home where animals weren't allowed. (You won't catch me in one of them!) One day there was a poor little guy, a poodle (not what I would have chosen), and he looked so miserable. His owner had died, and he looked so bewildered. You could see he didn't know what could have happened for him to end up surrounded by noisy dogs, and without his home comforts and someone to share his bed. After a while I spent so much time with him that I was 'persuaded' that I should adopt him. He was 10 years old. He was called Petal but I called him Pete. He didn't seem to mind. And that's how Chipper's legacy, as I call it, started. I had Pete for three years until he lost the will to live and I let him go. Then came Carter. I had him four years.

It was always the old ones. I didn't feel I was betraying Chipper, I felt like I was doing what he wanted. I took both dogs and cats, as long as they were old. I've had 10 now, counting the current one.

I loved this story, because I, too, am always drawn to the old dogs. I feel so bad for them when they've been having a nice life and then find themselves dumped into kennels, through no fault of their own, but usually due to the illness or passing of their owner. They must be so bewildered and think they must have done something wrong. So, do spare a thought for the 'oldies'.

CHAPTER 11

Spirit Messages

There should be no doubt in your mind by now that dogs and cats have just as much of a place in heaven as we do. I'm convinced that we'll be reunited with the pets we have loved, just as we will be with the people. So, it's no surprise to me that dogs and cats sometimes come back to bring through messages from a lost loved one or, sometimes, themselves. Just as has always been the case with our beloved animal friends, they love to serve us and other members of their 'pack', and bringing through messages is just one way they do that.

You might ask why passed-over loved ones would use the spirit of a cat or a dog to send us a message. I have a theory. In the case of ghostly visitations, I think one of the reasons is that most of us (even if we don't like to admit it) would be profoundly disturbed at seeing, hearing or feeling a passed-over person. Whereas being confronted with a friendly pet – in any shape or form – doesn't frighten us or cause any unpleasant feelings. Our loved ones, as thoughtful as ever, often choose pets they have been reunited with to communicate with us, although they do also sometimes come through themselves, but with an animal companion to reassure us.

The reason our passed-over loved ones send messages through our living pets, rather than directly to us, is also obvious to me. In many ways animals are more spiritual than people and, therefore, more innately wise of the ways of spirit and more susceptible to 'hearing' the message that's being sent through.

Mary's story

I had just graduated from business school in Syracuse, NY. I had had an apartment all lined up to share with several of my house-mates; I had had an interview for a good job at Syracuse Medical Center all set up; my life was just beginning. Then Dad told me he wanted me to come home because my mother needed me. I adored my father, so his wish was my command, even though I could not understand his request. My mother and I didn't see eye-to-eye very well (she had always been extremely controlling), and I just didn't see her needing me... but, I did as my father requested.

I got my very first job at Cornell University working in the Equine Research facility, which was just being built. I had only been there a week when my father passed away, leaving me to cope with our farm, my mother, my new job and the insanity of it all. My father passed away in August and was buried the day before my 19th birthday. I finally understood why my mother needed me.

During the next nine months, I sold off the farm animals and most of the farm equipment because my mother had major surgery, followed by a nervous breakdown. I managed to hang on to my job though, and I grieved over the loss of my father. I could hardly bear to go through each day without his strength and his support. I missed him horribly, and because of his death, my life had totally changed direction. I had to grow up fast. I became the person on whom my mother depended to keep her world straight, but she quickly went back to being a control freak and

I hated it. It had all happened so quickly – in the flash of an eye. One day the following spring, I was standing at the window at the top of the staircase looking out across the back yard at the empty barns and the unplanted gardens, crying, still mourning the loss of my father. Suddenly, my father appeared to me in 3D. He was wearing his overalls and boots and he walked across the back yard towards the cow barn. My collie dog, Smokey (also deceased) was walking along beside him just like he had always done when I wasn't around. My dad got directly across from the open window and stopped. He looked up at me and smiled, looking directly into my eyes. Dad turned and continued on towards the barn, he and my dog fading into the daylight. I was stunned. My dog had brought my Dad to see me! They were together! Then suddenly, I felt a rush of peace and comfort course through my body, while a warm feeling of love swept down from my head to my toes, sort of like the buzz from a gentle electrical current. It was euphoric. Then it all went away as quickly as had come. In its stead, it left a sensation, a feeling, a knowledge, if you will, that my father was happy where he was and that I should stop grieving for him. From that day forward, I knew my father was only a heartbeat away, that he would always be with me and that my life would be just fine.

I've had many encounters with Spirit in my lifetime, some good, some not so good, some wonderful. My dad and my angels have been with me all of my life. My father came to escort my mother home a few years back. One day I will see them both again, and Smokey.

Mary was so lucky to see this amazing vision, which was able to assure her that her dog and her dad were still looking out for each other, so that she needn't worry about either of them.

Wendy's story

In the last lonely months of writing my PhD thesis, my husband gave me a little kitten, to keep me company in the long hours. She was very tiny and only six weeks old. She latched onto me immediately, accepting me as her new mother, and I was delighted with my little furry companion. We developed an incredible relationship. She followed me everywhere and 'helped' me with my chores, whether it was by sniffing at the laundry or jumping into a pile of raked leaves in the garden. Since I work mainly from home, she spent most of her waking hours with me. Whenever I thought to myself that I had not seen her for a while (which for us was anything more than an hour), she'd come through her cat door within two minutes of me having had that thought. I guess you could call it a psychic link. My husband called us Batman and Robin, because we were always together.

We're a German-speaking family so we named her Kati, which was short for the German word *Katze* or cat. When Kati was three years old I became pregnant. Halfway through the pregnancy my husband and I went away for a week, leaving Kati with a friend. During that week our friend called us to say that Kati was missing. We came home from the trip immediately. I'd had a disturbing dream the night before that she was missing, and it was terrifying that it had come true. Things had to be serious. We drove through the night and searched unsuccessfully for Kati all morning. In the late afternoon fatigue took over and I slept for an hour. I woke up knowing immediately where to find her. It was on the neighbouring property, which we could only access by climbing a fence. I found her quickly, just a few metres from our front door. She was dead. I was devastated, and a long and painful mourning process began.

Ten days after Kati's death, I went to the hospital to have a baby scan. The doctor, whom I'd never met before and who knew nothing of our family, asked if we had a name for the baby. We did, but in my sadness I told him no, simply because I didn't want to talk. He joked with me that the babies he scans 'talk' to him. He looked at me and said, 'Your baby is telling me her name. Do you want to know?' I didn't care. I only wanted my cat back, so I shrugged. He said, 'Her name is Kate.' I burst into tears and called my husband. I think the doctor was worried he had upset me, but that was far from the truth.

Five months later our daughter was born and we named her Kate. I don't know what it means and I don't want to speculate. Sometimes Kate is eerily similar in personality to Kati, however it just makes me smile, like she's saying hello to us from another place. Kati left a legacy much larger than her name. There's not a day goes by when I don't think about her, miss her, love her and thank her for gracing our lives.

Was Kate, Kati come back to life? Or did Kate bring through a message from Kati to make Wendy feel better? To be honest it could be either, but whichever it was, as long as it made her happy and relieved her grief, it was a job well done.

Paula's story

Ruby was a little black Patterdale Terrier with a white chest. She really belonged to my mam and dad, but I soon thought of her as mine, too. She was a little dog with a huge personality, and at times I'd swear she'd been here before. Sometimes it seemed like she'd try to have a conversation with me.

Last summer Ruby started having fits, foaming at the mouth, and it was a dreadful thing to see her little body swinging back and forth with her eyes rolling, and when she came out of it she didn't seem to know where she was. The first time I saw her fitting, I was in tears. I cradled her up, put her in my car and took her to the vet. She was diagnosed with epilepsy, and we had to treat her with small tablets. This treatment was successful until this year, when the fits started getting worse. She was confused, panting and going round in circles, yelping. The vet took her in and told me he'd ring or if anything changed. I went home.

Later on when I rang the vet, the nurse told me that Ruby was doing great. I was so happy and excited, but then while I was talking to the nurse I heard Ruby yelping. The phone was dropped, and when she came back I said, 'That was my Ruby, wasn't it?' There was a pause and then the nurse said, 'I'm so sorry. Ruby isn't as well as we thought. The computer hadn't updated her file properly.' My heart thumped and my tummy churned. I knew what she was saying and I said, 'I'm coming down. Don't let her go.' My sister took me and my daughter because I couldn't drive for crying.

I walked into the room, fighting back the tears with all my might. Ruby was sedated, but the vet said she'd still sense us there. A few minutes later and little Ruby was gone. I couldn't sleep, feeling guilty and as if I'd failed her. My dad helped me bury Ruby in the garden, and we planted some forget-me-nots, saying our last goodbyes. I drove towards home, thinking about Ruby and asking her for a sign that she was OK. Something made me turn the car around and go back. As I arrived at my mam's house I had an idea. I begged Ruby to bring me a bright red sky, to go with her name, to prove that she could hear me and she forgave me. I went to the grave and looked up. The sky right above was suddenly a deep crimson. My beautiful Ruby came through for me.

Angels do sometimes use natural beauty to send through a message. This is why I always say even if something is photo-shopped in some way to make it beautiful, if the soul sees it as beautiful then it still has the same effect of lifting the spirit, just like it did in Paula's case, when it was a true sign.

Jerry's story

My Mum was the centre of my world and when she died suddenly from a stroke, I was bereft. Dad had died years before and now I was alone. Nothing had any colour, nothing was worth doing. I sunk into depression. One afternoon I was sitting around on the sofa, snacking (I rarely had anything better to do) and I contemplated suicide. I resisted it, but the thoughts kept coming back. I snacked more. I got fatter. I got more miserable. I soon found myself on a vicious cycle downhill, getting progressively fatter and that made me even more miserable, so I ate to cheer myself up. I could almost, almost hear my mum's voice ticking me off. She would have hated how I'd let myself go. So I said to her, 'If you really care, come back to visit me.' Nothing. I made bargains with her, with God, I would promise to get back on track before I ate myself into a heart attack if I could just see Mum one more time. Nothing. Could it be that she didn't care about me anymore? Did God not care about me? If not, why should I care for myself?

I got to daydreaming back in time to when I was a kid. Something came to mind for some reason that I had never thought about before. I recalled that my Mum had had a cat called Tinker. I don't know why this cat came to mind. Then I got it. The cat had been really fat, a real porker. I remember Dad moaning that Mum had fed that cat better than him. It got lazier and lazier and I suppose there was a resemblance to me in the weight department. I couldn't really remember the cat much, I was quite young when it suddenly keeled over one day. Mum rushed it to the vet in a panic. I can remember being bundled round to the neighbour's. The cat made it home, but with dire warnings to Mum to get its weight down. She couldn't do it. The cat would cry for food and Mum would always give in. Two months later the cat disappeared. I guessed now, though no one said anything back then, that it had died. I know Mum cried a bit.

I sighed, goodness knows why I was thinking about this. I couldn't even think what colour it was and no cat was going to make me stop eating, even if it died from being overweight. I opened my eyes, and just for a second or two, like an after-image from a bright light, there was a cat standing right in front of the sofa! It was black with white bib and feet and, man, was it fat! Biggest cat I ever saw. Then it was gone, just like that.

In a fever now I raced upstairs and started raking through the boxes of photos in the wardrobe. They hadn't been looked at for years and years. I went on a journey back in time till I finally found me as a toddler – must have been 60 years ago. And finally, there it was – a shot of the cat. It was a bit faded, but there was the cat in the garden, and it looked exactly like the one I'd just seen… I must have stood there for 10 minutes not believing it. Finally, the photo slid from my hand and underneath, where it had been stuck to the back of the cat photo, was a photo of my Mum. It was taken one Christmas and she was messing around telling me there were no presents for me! She was shaking her finger at me, a mock frown on her face. She was looking right at me from the photograph. She was clearly telling me it was her fault the cat had died, and she wasn't going to let the same thing happen to me!

When I thought about the trouble my Mum must have gone to up there in Heaven to get this message to me, it stopped me in my tracks. Of course, she loved me and she must have been so upset at how I was wasting my life. So she sent me the fat cat to make me see sense! Well it worked...

This visitation not only changed Jerry's life but actually saved it, too! Was it his mum who engineered this, or the cat, or perhaps both of them working in perfect harmony?

CHAPTER 12

A Last Few Words and Some Fun

We have a responsibility to our pets that we don't really have to any other being. We have to accept that they are what they are and their nature is what it is. While on this Earth a cat or a dog may be your 'baby' and/or be known by a name that means the world to you. But behind that name they are also their breed and behind that their species. This means that however clever they may be, however charming and needed by you they are, and however spiritual they are, beneath that they have their own needs. If a cat or a dog cannot be itself through illness or old age, it isn't right to simply cling onto them as if they were an elderly person. A cat or a dog that cannot run or even walk, that cannot see or hear their owner, that cannot play with companions, or any of its toys, also cannot dull their pain or occupy their mind with reading, watching the TV, having a conversation, and therefore, in kindness to them, we must recognize the point at which we need to let them go, to let them move on, no matter what the cost to ourselves. Letting go of someone you love is that hardest thing in the world, but we prove our love by doing do.

When this time comes for you, be with them if you possibly can, be brave for them, though it breaks your heart. Don't let them be afraid by seeing you made to break down. Always remember that animals are the world's best empaths and will read your energy as you read a book. The thing is though, when you have a relationship with one of these very special cats or dogs, it is likely that they are actually a 'spark of your own soul'. This means they are connected to you on a deep and spiritual level. Not only have you most likely lived other lifetimes with this pet, but when they pass, you literally lose a part of your own soul, a part of you. No wonder then that the pain is so intense. So, when you let such a pet go, never feel guilty about it or try to suppress your feelings to suit other people who've never experienced what you're going through.

The good news is that, because you are connected on such a deep level, you are in fact never really parted at all; it just feels that way to your mortal self. These animals will almost always stay around you in spirit and if you open your mind to the little clues, you'll have plenty of evidence of it. Also, they will most likely come back to you in another body, sometimes in this life or sometimes in future lives. So, be comforted.

My main fear when I lost my beloved Ace was that being next to me was so important to her in life that I was terrified her spirit would be lost without me, unable to find me and in as much pain without me as I was without her. Of course, now I know that was never the case because her soul is tethered to mine as securely as a boat to its mooring. She was with a spirit part of me as soon as she took her last breath. She could never really be lost – and neither can your pet.

Now it's time to move on to the fun part!

Your Dog's Sign of the Zodiac

ARIES dogs like to be the pack leader, so make sure you stay in charge in every situation. Aries dogs are born winners and make good show dogs because of this. They are usually fearless and this can get them into trouble, so if your dog is small make sure he doesn't take on the school bully, thinking he's bigger than he is. These dogs will always forgive you and don't hold grudges.

TAURUS dogs love to be pampered. They will always want the best seat in front of the fire. The key to a happy life with a Taurus dog is to always let them think they've won. Persuade them that everything is their idea and you can't go wrong. They are very loving and make the ideal dog if you love a cuddle, and they will sit for hours watching TV with you.

GEMINI dogs are always trying to communicate with their owners. They will sit in on a conversation among the family, trying desperately to understand what's going on. They can therefore be taught a huge vocabulary. Tell them everything that's going on, even if they can't understand, because if they feel left out they won't be happy. Because they like to talk they need training to stop them barking.

CANCER dogs love to be at home. They're the sort that will pull you home from a walk towards warmth and security, rather than when you set off. If you're late home for their walk, they will just sleep and wait patiently, so they're ideal for a busy person. These dogs make wonderful guardians and will be the sort to learn to nanny a baby.

LEO dogs think they are royalty and will love being groomed, pampered and having their teeth cleaned. They'll love sparkly, 'bling-type' collars and wear them with pride. They don't like being covered in mud, so if they do get dirty be sure to clean them off if you don't want them drying themselves on your white duvet cover. If you like to spend hours doing your hair and applying makeup, you'll love this dog.

VIRGO dogs don't need bathing as much as other dogs, because they do a lot of washing themselves. They also will often even nibble their own nails to save you having to trim them. They will be 'lickers' so you'll need to enjoy this form of doggy affection. They will quickly learn to put toys in a box when you want to clean up, and they are often one of those rare dogs that will actually like the vacuum cleaner.

LIBRA dogs are usually very attractive. They have the prettiest faces and well-proportioned bodies. They're not vain, though, and will be surprisingly 'roughie toughie' when required. These dogs will happily accompany you for hours on very long walks, and don't mind getting their paws dirty. With this kind of dog on the leash, be prepared for people to stop you to compliment him.

SCORPIO These dogs never grow up. They'll still love to play even in their dotage. Their favourite game would be 'hide and seek', where you hide their favourite toy and they go to look for it. You'll have to get clever with the hiding though, as they are as intelligent as they are fun. If you love a dog that will fetch for hours, even if he wasn't bred for it, then this is the right one for you. If you're a couch potato, this dog will insist you take on a whole new fitness regime.

SAGITTARIUS These dogs like to walk, not necessarily run, but walk. They love to explore new places and new neighbourhoods. If you don't walk them enough you might find you have an escape artist on your hands. Natural performers, these will make the best TV and film dogs and will happily let the kids play with them. They'll put up with anything for the sake of attention and exercise.

CAPRICORN This dog loves routine, but they are also very quick to learn. They make the best working dogs, whether it's in agility classes or rounding up sheep. They have active minds and get bored easily, so their routine should include a lot of diversity. If they 'help' you with chores like putting out the bins or feeding livestock, then they won't relax until all the jobs are done. Only then will they chill out.

AQUARIUS A very friendly dog, he'll really enjoy playing with others of his kind. He'll refuse to bark at anyone, and may lick a burglar to death, so if a watchdog is what you need, you'll have to get another dog to go with this one. They make good therapy dogs and will speak to everyone in a retirement home or a hospital. They also make good guide dogs and can do any type of job that involves helping people.

PISCES These dogs are very considerate and will the first to comfort you if they sense you're distressed. When you need a kiss or a cuddle, they will be there. These are the sort of dogs that you see in films, bringing someone help if they've been foolish enough to fall down a well, but for real. They will also play mum for any baby animals that might come into the house.

Your Cat's Sign of the Zodiac

ARIES All cats know their own minds, but this is especially true of the Aries cat. A bit free with his claws if tested, but he will still be happy to have the occasional snuggle with you on the sofa. Don't try and keep this mini-lion indoors or you will end up with shredded furniture, because he's a born hunter. This is a cat that will enjoy being trained, so make sure you acknowledge his intelligence. The devil will make work for idle paws!

TAURUS This is the couch potato of the cat world, so if you want a friend who's always happy to give you their full attention, this is the right one for you. Ignore him though at your peril, be late with his food and he'll sulk. This cat is quite vain, too, and one of the few who will really appreciate a sparkling, bling-covered collar. He can be an expensive cat because if you feed him salmon and caviar, that's what he'll come to expect.

GEMINI This will be a noisy cat. If you don't understand what he wants, you'll have to learn a lot of cat vocabulary in order to stop his yowling. Very demanding, he'll also be very loving, and repay your attention many times over. However, he'll have his 'I want to be alone' moments, too, so try to respect that. He won't be happy being an 'only cat', so it would be a good idea to get a companion, but make sure it's a more laid-back type, like a Taurus.

CANCER This cat will make your home his castle, and if you have to have an indoor cat, this is the best one for that. These cats will be fierce guards, and are the sort to have if you live in the wilderness and are threatened with bears! No attacker will be too big for this boy, and he'll even see off the odd foolish burglar.

LEO These cats often come through with high-maintenance, long coats. There is nothing as miserable as a Leo cat whose coat had been allowed to get filthy and matted. If fact, if you don't look after him properly (in his opinion, that is) he will up and leave, and go in search of someone who does. A Leo cat will exercise the pounds away and never be a 'fat cat', so if you like a cat whose appearance will do you proud, this is the right one for you.

VIRGO This cat will spend hours grooming himself, and will be a little aloof to mere humans. If you allow his litter box to get dirty, then beware, as he won't be above finding a little secret place to hide his droppings – and that might just be your shoe! On the upside this cat is the healer of the feline world and will be the first one of the family to notice if you're feeling a bit down.

LIBRA cats are usually very attractive. They have the prettiest faces and well-proportioned bodies. They're not vain though and will be surprisingly resilient and even ferocious when required. These cats will hunt for hours and, not being afraid of much, will bring home anything up to the size of an adult rabbit, so don't get one if you're squeamish.

SCORPIO These cats are forever kittenish. They'll still love to play even in their dotage. And they love to play-act, so toys on a string that you can manipulate less obviously will thrill them. This cat is quick and clever and won't let you enjoy too much of the peaceful life, always needing new adventures to stimulate him, so there will be few nights dreaming on the sofa for you as their owner. The right sort of cats to train, they will often learn to 'fetch'.

SAGITTARIUS These cats will always be out on the prowl, constantly exploring the far reaches of the neighbourhood. This means they can't be house cats and will need to be accepted as the free spirits they are. If you're a worrier who likes their cat to be home at a regular time, this isn't the star sign for you. However, they're very laid back in some respects, and will let kids and puppies pull them around with great tolerance.

CAPRICORN These cats will always want feeding at the same time, and any deviation in routine will upset them, so they will be inclined to train *you*. They love their owners with a passion and will want to follow them everywhere, even to the bathroom, where they'll love to dabble in the water trickling from a tap. Fun-loving and companionable, they are great company.

AQUARIUS This cat will love everyone and never let a growl pass his lips. Sunny and charming, he'll make friends easily. This is a good therapy cat and can be trained to visit hospital patients and people in homes to cheer them up. He can be relied on never to bite or scratch, so if you have a rodent problem he probably won't be much help. He doesn't show devotion to any one person, so don't get one if you want a personal friend to talk to.

PISCES This cat is the ideal companion that will sit and be cuddled and talked to for hours, and show rapt attention if you are distressed. He will accept any amount of other waifs and strays into the home and will play 'mum' to kittens, puppies and babies alike. Unable to sit by in the face of unhappiness, he's quite likely to turn himself into a clown in order to amuse.

Your Dog or Cat's Name

Evidence I've had suggests that even very small changes in a pet's name can alter his behaviour. Numerology gives insight into whether your cat has the right name.

Use this chart to find what number your dog or cat's name reduces to.

1	2	3	4	5	6	7	8	9
A	B	C	D	E	F	G	H	I
J	K	L	M	N	O	P	Q	R
S	T	U	V	W	X	Y	Z	

Keep adding the digits together until you reach a single figure. For instance, CHLOE would be 3 + 8 + 3 + 6 + 5 which = 25 and 2 + 5 = 7, so this name has a value of 7.

1. This will encourage a pet to have a need for adventure, so if you want a house dog or cat, this name will need to be changed.

2. This number will mean the dog or cat should love nothing better than a cuddle in front of a roaring fire, so the indoor life could suit them.

3. This dog or cat will be bright and intelligent and also a bit messy, so be ready for lots of shredded curtains or dead prey 'gifts' around the house.

4. This dog or cat will like to know exactly when everything is going to happen and will 'nag' incessantly when things (or you) are late.

5. This pet will be a bundle of fun, always up for a game, even when you're too tired to co-operate. Plenty of brain work will be needed to calm him down.

6. This dog or cat will treat everyone the same, so he's not the one for someone who values loyalty in their pet above all else.

7. This dog or cat is very sensitive and will require gentle handling at all times, so you'll need lots of patience.

8. This dog or cat wants to learn and needs new tricks and toys to be introduced every week or he'll get bored and find his own fun.

9. This pet can be strong and wilful, so change the name if you don't want to be constantly battling. If you enjoy a challenge, you'll be fine.

If you'd like to change your dog or cat a little, try changing a few letters in his name and see what happens. For instance, Chloe could become Callie, which would change the value from a 7 to a 6 and might encourage your pet to become more gregarious and less sensitive.

Resources

I've been given permission by Penelope Smith to include here her code of ethics, which, in my opinion, all communicators with animals should be bound by.

Code of Ethics for Interspecies Telepathic Communicators

Formulated in 1990 by Penelope Smith (www.animaltalk.net)

Our motivation is compassion for all beings and a desire to help all species understand each other better, particularly to help restore the lost human ability to freely and directly communicate with other species.

We honour those that come to us for help, not judging, condemning or invalidating them for their mistakes or misunderstanding, but honouring their desire for change and harmony.

We know that to keep this work as pure and harmonious as possible requires that we continually grow spiritually. We realize that telepathic communication can be clouded or overlaid by our own unfulfilled emotions, critical judgments or lack of love for self and others. We walk in humility, willing to recognize and clear up our own errors in understanding others' communication (human and non-human alike).

We cultivate knowledge and understanding of the dynamics of human, non-human and interspecies behaviour and relationships, to increase the good results of our work. We get whatever education and/or personal help we need to do our work effectively, with compassion, respect, joy and harmony.

We seek to draw out the best in everyone and increase understanding towards mutual resolution of problems. We go only where we are asked to help, so that others are receptive and we truly can assist. We respect the feelings and ideas of others and work for interspecies understanding, not pitting one side against another, but walking with compassion for all. We acknowledge the things that we cannot change and continue where our work can be most effective.

We respect the privacy of people and animal companions we work with and honour their desire for confidentiality.

While doing our best to help, we allow others their own dignity and help them to help their animal companions. We cultivate understanding and ability in others, rather than dependence on our ability. We offer people ways to be involved in understanding and growth with their fellow beings of other species.

We acknowledge our limitations, seeking help from other professionals as needed. It is not our job to name and treat diseases, and we refer people to veterinarians for diagnosis of physical illness. We may relay animals' ideas, feelings, pains, symptoms, as they describe them or as we feel or perceive them, and this may be helpful to veterinary health professionals. We may also assist through handling of stresses, counselling, and other gentle healing methods. We let clients decide for themselves how to work with healing their animal companions' distress, disease or injury, given all the information available.

The goal of any consultation, lecture, workshop or interspecies experience is more communication, balance, compassion, understanding and communion among all beings. We follow our heart, honouring the spirit and life of all beings as One.

Animal Communicators

www.centaur-therapies.co.uk

www.valheart.com

www.animalenergy.com

www.animaltalk.net/animalcommunicatordirectory.htm

www.animalpsychic.co.uk

www.talktotheanimals.co.uk

www.animalmagictraining.com

www.shininghorse.co.uk/about-susie

www.sarah-janepetwhisperer.com/about-sarah-jane

www.petsofthehomeless.org

www.animaltranslations.com

www.animalthoughts.com

www.animalscantalk2me.com

www.carolschultz.com

www.petsastherapy.org

If you care about the plight of animals, please join my friend Brian May in his quest here: www.save-me.org.uk

YouTube videos

Here are some links to videos that you'll enjoy and that may astound you:

Animal odd couple, a dog and an elephant: http://tinyurl.com/7t2tzr

A dog and a lion are friends: http://tinyurl.com/caljrs

A monkey raises a kitten: http://tinyurl.com/y9shvzsx

Tiger cubs are fed by a pig: http://tinyurl.com/yb6pheh9

ABOUT THE AUTHOR

Tony Smedley

Since the age of two, **Jenny Smedley** has enjoyed a spiritual connection with animals which, over the years, has grown to full communication with them. Now based in the beautiful, open countryside of Norfolk, in the UK, Jenny lives with her husband and soulmate of 50 years, Tony, and her several times reincarnated dog. Their acre garden is mostly a wildlife habitat, very bee-, butterfly- and other pollinator-friendly, and full of secret little areas where birds, deer, partridges, pheasants, foxes and hedgehogs make their nests and homes in safety. The large wildlife pond she and Tony created is home to frogs, toads, newts and stickleback fish, as well as many and varied beetles and insects, including magnificent dragonflies.

She's been an author, TV and radio presenter/guest, angel artist, international columnist and spiritual consultant. Her own current life was turned around by a vision from her one of her own past lives. Jenny has appeared on many TV shows and hundreds of radio shows around the world, including in the UK, USA, Australia, Tasmania, New Zealand, the Caribbean, South Africa, Iceland and Spain.

 JennySmedleyAngelWhisperer

 @SmedleyJenny

 author@globalnet.co.uk

www.jennysmedley.co.uk

Notes

Notes

HAY HOUSE

Look within

Join the conversation about latest products,
events, exclusive offers and more.

  Hay House UK

  @HayHouseUK

  @hayhouseuk

  healyourlife.com

We'd love to hear from you!